BLACK AMERICAN POETS
AND DRAMATISTS
BEFORE THE HARLEM RENAISSANCE

Writers of English: Lives and Works

BLACK AMERICAN POETS AND DRAMATISTS

BEFORE THE HARLEM RENAISSANCE

Edited and with an Introduction by

Harold Bloom

092678

CHELSEA HOUSE PUBLISHERS
New York   Philadelphia

Jacket illustration: Anonymous engraving of Phillis Wheatley in *Poems on Various Subjects, Religious and Moral* (London: Printed for Archibald Bell & sold in Boston by Cox & Berry, 1773) (courtesy Library of Congress).

CHELSEA HOUSE PUBLISHERS

Editorial Director Richard Rennert
Executive Managing Editor Karyn Gullen Browne
Picture Editor Adrian G. Allen
Copy Chief Robin James
Art Director Robert Mitchell
Manufacturing Director Gerald Levine

Writers of English: Lives and Works

Senior Editor S. T. Joshi
Series Design Rae Grant

Staff for BLACK AMERICAN POETS AND DRAMATISTS BEFORE THE HARLEM RENAISSANCE

Research Robert Green
Editorial Assistant Mary Sisson

First Printing

1 3 5 7 9 8 6 4 2

Library of Congress Cataloging-in-Publication Data

Black American poets and dramatists: before the Harlem renaissance / edited and with an introduction by Harold Bloom.
    p. cm.—(Writers of English)
    Includes bibliographical references.
    ISBN 0-7910-2205-6.—ISBN 0-7910-2230-7 (pbk.)
  1. American literature—Afro-American authors—Bio-bibliography. 2. American literature—Afro-American authors—Dictionaries. 3. Afro-Americans—Intellectual life—Dictionaries. 4. Afro-Americans in literature—Dictionaries. I. Bloom, Harold. II. Series.
PS153.N5B533 1994   93-8344
810.9′896073—dc20   CIP
[B]

▨ Contents

❖ User's Guide

THIS VOLUME PROVIDES biographical, critical, and bibliographical information on the twelve most significant black American poets and dramatists up to the early twentieth century. Each chapter consists of three parts: a biography of the author; a selection of brief critical extracts about the author; and a bibliography of the author's published books.

The biography supplies a detailed outline of the important events in the author's life, including his or her major writings. The critical extracts are taken from a wide array of books and periodicals, from the author's lifetime to the present, and range in content from biographical to critical to historical. The extracts are arranged in chronological order by date of writing or publication, and a full bibliographical citation is provided at the end of each extract. Editorial additions or deletions are indicated within carets.

The author bibliographies list every separate publication—including books, pamphlets, broadsides, collaborations, and works edited or translated by the author—for works published in the author's lifetime; selected important posthumous publications are also listed. Titles are those of the first edition; if a work has subsequently come to be known under a variant title, this title is supplied within carets. In selected instances dates of revised editions are given where these are significant. Pseudonymous works are listed, but the pseudonyms under which these works were published are not. Periodicals edited by the author are listed only when the author has written most or all of the contents. For plays we have listed date of publication, not date of production; unpublished plays are not listed. Titles enclosed in square brackets are of doubtful authenticity. All works by the author, whether in English or in other languages, have been listed; English translations of foreign-language works are not listed unless the author has done the translation.

The Life of the Author

Harold Bloom

NIETZSCHE, WITH EXULTANT ANGUISH, famously proclaimed that God was dead. Whatever the consequences of this for the ethical life, its ultimate literary effect certainly would have surprised the author Nietzsche. His French disciples, Foucault most prominent among them, developed the Nietzschean proclamation into the dogma that all authors, God included, were dead. The death of the author, which is no more than a Parisian trope, another metaphor for fashion's setting of skirt-lengths, is now accepted as literal truth by most of our current apostles of what should be called French Nietzsche, to distinguish it from the merely original Nietzsche. We also have French Freud or Lacan, which has little to do with the actual thought of Sigmund Freud, and even French Joyce, which interprets *Finnegans Wake* as the major work of Jacques Derrida. But all this is as nothing compared to the final triumph of the doctrine of the death of the author: French Shakespeare. That delicious absurdity is given us by the New Historicism, which blends Foucault and California fruit juice to give us the Word that Renaissance "social energies," and not William Shakespeare, composed *Hamlet* and *King Lear*. It seems a proper moment to murmur "enough" and to return to a study of the life of the author.

Sometimes it troubles me that there are so few masterpieces in the vast ocean of literary biography that stretches between James Boswell's great *Life* of Dr. Samuel Johnson and the late Richard Ellmann's wonderful *Oscar Wilde*. Literary biography is a crucial genre, and clearly a difficult one in which to excel. The actual nature of the lives of the poets seems to have little effect upon the quality of their biographies. Everything happened to Lord Byron and nothing at all to Wallace Stevens, and yet their biographers seem equally daunted by them. But even inadequate biographies of strong writers, or of weak ones, are of immense use. I have never read a literary biography from which I have not profited, a statement I cannot make about any other genre whatsoever. And when it comes to figures who are central to us—Dante, Shakespeare, Cervantes, Montaigne, Goethe, Whitman, Tolstoi, Freud, Joyce, Kafka among them—we reach out eagerly for every scrap that the biographers have gleaned. Concerning Dante and Shakespeare we know much too little, yet when we come to Goethe and Freud, where we seem to know more than everything, we still want to know more. The death of the author, despite our current resentniks, clearly was only a momentary fad. Something vital in every authentic lover of literature responds to Emerson's battle-cry sentence: "There is no history, only biography." Beyond that there is a deeper truth, difficult to come at and requiring a lifetime to understand, which is that there is no literature, only autobiography, however mediated, however veiled, however transformed. The events of Shakespeare's life included the composition of *Hamlet,* and that act of writing was itself a crucial act of living, though we do not yet know altogether how to read so doubled an act. When an author takes up a more overtly autobiographical stance, as so many do in their youth, again we still do not know precisely how to accommodate the vexed relation between life and work. T. S. Eliot, meditating upon James Joyce, made a classic statement as to such accommodation:

> We want to know who are the originals of his characters, and what were
> the origins of his episodes, so that we may unravel the web of memory
> and invention and discover how far and in what ways the crude material
> has been transformed.

When a writer is not even covertly autobiographical, the web of memory and invention is still there, but so subtly woven that we may never unravel it. And yet we want deeply never to stop trying, and not merely because we are curious, but because each of us is caught in her own network of memory and invention. We do not always recall our inventions, and long before we age we cease to be certain of the extent to which we have invented our memories. Perhaps one motive for reading is our need to unravel our own webs. If our masters could make, from their lives, what we read, then we can be moved by them to ask: What have we made or lived in relation to what we have read? The answers may be sad, or confused, but the question is likely, implicitly, to go on being asked as long as we read. In Freudian terms, we are asking: What is it that we have repressed? What have we forgotten, unconsciously but purposely: What is it that we flee? Art, literature necessarily included, is regression in the service of the ego, according to a famous Freudian formula. I doubt the Freudian wisdom here, but indubitably it is profoundly suggestive. When we read, something in us keeps asking the equivalent of the Freudian questions: From what or whom is the author in flight, and to what earlier stages in her life is she returning, and why?

Reading, whether as an art or a pastime, has been damaged by the visual media, television in particular, and might be in some danger of extinction in the age of the computer, except that the psychic need for it continues to endure, presumably because it alone can assuage a central loneliness in elitist society. Despite all sophisticated or resentful denials, the reading of imaginative literature remains a quest to overcome the isolation of the individual consciousness. We can read for information, or entertainment, or for love of the language, but in the end we seek, in the author, the person whom we have not found, whether in ourselves or in others. In that quest, there always are elements at once aggressive and defensive, so that reading, even in childhood, is rarely free of hidden anxieties. And yet it remains one of the few activities not contaminated by an entropy of spirit. We read in hope, because we lack companionship, and the author can become the object of the most idealistic elements in our search for the wit and inventiveness we so desperately require. We read biography, not as a supplement to reading the author, but as a second, fresh attempt to understand what always seems to evade us in the work, our drive towards a kind of identity with the author.

This will-to-identity, though recently much deprecated, is a prime basis for the experience of sublimity in reading. *Hamlet* retains its unique position in the Western canon not because most readers and playgoers identify themselves with the prince, who clearly is beyond them, but rather because they find themselves again in the power of the language that represents him with such immediacy and force. Yet we know that neither language nor social energy created Hamlet. Our curiosity about Shakespeare is endless, and never will be appeased. That curiosity itself is a value, and cannot be separated from the value of *Hamlet* the tragedy, or Hamlet the literary character. It provokes us that Shakespeare the man seems so unknowable, at once everyone and no one as Borges shrewdly observes. Critics keep telling us otherwise, yet something valid in us keeps believing that we would know Hamlet better if Shakespeare's life were as fully known as the lives of Goethe and Freud, Byron and Oscar Wilde, or best of all, Dr. Samuel Johnson. Shakespeare never will have his Boswell, and Dante never will have his Richard Ellmann. How much one would give for a detailed and candid *Life of Dante* by Petrarch, or an outspoken memoir of Shakespeare by Ben Jonson! Or, in the age just past, how superb would be rival studies of one another by Hemingway and Scott Fitzgerald! But the list is endless: think of *Oscar Wilde* by Lord Alfred Douglas, or a joint biography of Shelley by Mary Godwin, Emilia Viviani, and Jane Williams. More than our insatiable desire for scandal would be satisfied. The literary rivals and the lovers of the great writers possessed perspectives we will never enjoy, and without those perspectives we dwell in some poverty in regard to the writers with whom we ourselves never can be done.

There is a sense in which imaginative literature *is* perspectivism, so that the reader is likely to be overwhelmed by the work's difficulty unless its multiple perspectives are mastered. Literary biography matters most because it is a storehouse of perspectives, frequently far surpassing any that are grasped by the particular biographer. There are relations between authors' lives and their works of kinds we have yet to discover, because our analytical instruments are not yet advanced enough to perform the necessary labor. Perhaps a novel, poem, or play is not so much a regression in the service of the ego, as it is an amalgam of *all* the Freudian mechanisms of defense, all working together for the apotheosis of the ego. Freud valued art highly, but thought that the aesthetic enterprise was no rival for psychoanalysis, unlike religion and philosophy. Clearly Freud was mistaken; his own anxieties about his indebtedness to Shakespeare helped produce the weirdness of his joining in the lunacy that argued for the Earl of Oxford as the author of

Shakespeare's plays. It was Shakespeare, and not "the poets," who was there before Freud arrived at his depth psychology, and it is Shakespeare who is there still, well out ahead of psychoanalysis. We see what Freud would not see, that psychoanalysis is Shakespeare prosified and systematized. Freud is part of literature, not of "science," and the biography of Freud has the same relations to psychoanalysis as the biography of Shakespeare has to *Hamlet* and *King Lear,* if only we knew more of the life of Shakespeare.

Western literature, particularly since Shakespeare, is marked by the representation of internalized change in its characters. A literature of the ever-growing inner self is in itself a large form of biography, even though this is the biography of imaginary beings, from Hamlet to the sometimes nameless protagonists of Kafka and Beckett. Skeptics might want to argue that all literary biography concerns imaginary beings, since authors make themselves up, and every biographer gives us a creation curiously different from the same author as seen by the writer of a rival *Life.* Boswell's Johnson is not quite anyone else's Johnson, though it is now very difficult for us to disentangle the great Doctor from his gifted Scottish friend and follower. The life of the author is not merely a metaphor or a fiction, as is "the Death of the Author," but it always does contain metaphorical or fictive elements. Those elements are a part of the value of literary biography, but not the largest or the crucial part, which is the separation of the mask from the man or woman who hid behind it. James Joyce and Samuel Beckett, master and sometime disciple, were both of them enigmatic personalities, and their biographers have not, as yet, fully expounded the mystery of these contrasting natures. Beckett seems very nearly to have been a secular saint: personally disinterested, heroic in the French Resistance, as humane a person ever to have composed major fictions and dramas. Joyce, self-obsessed even as Beckett was preternaturally selfless, was the Milton of the twentieth century. Beckett was perhaps the least egoistic post-Joycean, post-Proustian, post-Kafkan of writers. Does that illuminate the problematical nature of his work, or does it simply constitute another problem? Whatever the cause, the question matters. The only death of the author that is other than literal, and that matters, is the fate only of weak writers. The strong, who become canonical, never die, which is what the canon truly is about. To be read forever is the Life of the Author.

⊕ Introduction

PAUL LAURENCE DUNBAR, greatly esteemed as a poet in his own brief lifetime (he died at thirty-three, of tuberculosis and alcoholic complications), seems today the major African-American poet before Sterling Brown and Robert Hayden. A writer rarely has been appreciated by so diverse a body of admirers as Dunbar: his circle of readers included President Theodore Roosevelt, Secretary of State John Hay, the novelist William Dean Howells, the English composer Samuel Coleridge-Taylor, the poets James Whitcomb Riley and James Weldon Johnson, and the most prominent black leaders: Booker T. Washington, W. E. B. DuBois, and Frederick Douglass. Reading through Dunbar's *Complete Poems* now, one sees why his early appeal was so universal, despite his limitations. Whether he writes in dialect or not, his concerns are central and traditional while his emphasis and accent are individual, to a surprising degree. I have been haunted for years by his agonistic meditation, "The Mystery," where the honesty of a desperate spirit's quest issues in a strong closure:

> I question of th' eternal bending skies
> That seem to neighbor with the novice earth;
> But they roll on and daily shut their eyes
> On me, as I one day shall do on them,
> And tell me not the secret that I ask.

Shelley's agnosticism is alluded to earlier, in the poem's deliberate echo of "To a Skylark": "I fain would look before / And after, but can neither do." Dunbar frequently writes variations upon Shelley, whose skepticism seems to me the dominant poetic influence upon the first major African-American poet. The celebrated lyric, "We Wear the Mask," blends an analysis of apparent black good humor with a Shelleyan ontological lament that transcends social injustice without neglecting its pervasiveness. Dunbar's lyric masterpiece in the Shelleyan mode of Promethean complaint in his hypnotic "Ere Sleep Comes Down to Soothe the Weary Eyes," a poem that Shelley (and Poe) would have admired, and yet also might have seen as Dunbar's tragic failure to cast out remorse, a polemic crucial to Shelley's battle against Christian morality. Something permanently poignant in Dunbar's poetry results from the conflict between his acceptance of the Promethean denunciation of remorse, and his cultural sensitivity to suffering and pain. Bitterness, diagnosed by Shelley as a consequence of remorse, informs some of Dunbar's most powerful poems, including his tribute to Robert Gould Shaw, who led the black 54th Massachusetts Regiment in the assault upon Fort Wagner (near Charleston) in July 1863, an attack of outrageous courage that destroyed Shaw and half his command. Dunbar's skepticism as to the value of the sacrifice is conveyed rather more indirectly in "The Colored Soldiers," where he asserts that "the Blacks enjoy their freedom, / And they won it dearly, too."

In what may be his most famous lyric, "Sympathy" popularized by Maya Angelou's use of the first lines of its final stanza: "I know why the caged bird sings"), Dunbar's conflicts achieve an apotheosis. The poem's movement is from empathy with the imprisoned bird, a knowledge of feeling, through a more savage knowledge of self-destructiveness, on to a knowledge of metaphor or poetic language itself. To have an understanding of the relationship between suffering and song is to enter again into Shelley's skeptical dialectic in which good and the means of good are irreconcilable. Like his precursor Shelley, Dunbar had a tragic awareness of the limits of art, and a keen apprehension of the triumph of life over lyrical intensity and individual integrity. Dunbar paradoxically prefigures the Shelleyan quests of Hart Crane and of the Robert Hayden of *Middle Passage*, in which the shadowing of poetic language by the sorrows of history engenders a strain by which the lyrical temperament is at once impaired yet also spurred on to an achievement near the limits of lyric.

—H. B.

William Stanley Braithwaite
1878–1962

WILLIAM STANLEY BRAITHWAITE was born in Boston on December 26, 1878, the son of Emma De Wolfe and William Smith Braithwaite. His father, who was from a distinguished West Indian family, educated the Braithwaite children in the genteel atmosphere of their home. Upon the death of the elder Braithwaite, William Stanley, now in his eighth year, began to attend school. His formal education came to an end four years later when his desire to help support his family led to an apprenticeship at Ginn & Company, where he was exposed to the world of books. Braithwaite made frequent trips to the Boston Public Library to educate himself.

In June 1903 Braithwaite married Emma Kelly, with whom he had seven children. His first volume of poetry, *Lyrics of Life and Love*, was published in 1904 and reflected the influence of the English Romantic poets, especially Keats and Shelley. Although Braithwaite favorably reviewed many poets who used nontraditional poetic language and devices, his own poetry was, for the most part, marked by technical precision and recognizable literary influences. His poems continued to be published in magazines and journals such as *New England Magazine*, *American Magazine*, *Voice*, *Century*, *Atlantic Monthly*, and *Book News Monthly*. In 1908 his second collection of verse, *The House of Falling Leaves*, was published. The volume showed an increasing attraction toward the sonnet as well as a tendency toward mysticism—possibly a reflection of Braithwaite's interest in William Blake—and included many pieces in celebration of particular persons. Though he was not insensitive to the plight of fellow black American writers, Braithwaite's early poetry was not influenced by, or concerned with, issues of race.

The depth of Braithwaite's interest in poetry was manifested in his emergence as a leading critic of verse. The influence of his columns in the *Boston Transcript*, articles in black periodicals, and the appearance of his *Poetry Journal* in 1912 (a short-lived enterprise that lasted only until 1914) inspired W. E. B. Du Bois to call Braithwaite "the most prominent critic of poetry in America." Braithwaite did much to foster new American poets, especially those of African-American heritage, and it became a coveted honor to have poems reviewed by him and included in his yearly anthologies, the first of which was the *Anthology of Magazine Verse for 1913*. These anthologies continued to appear until 1929; in 1959 appeared a new anthology, containing a selection from the seventeen previous volumes. Braithwaite also published *The Book of Elizabethan Verse* (1908), *The Book of Georgian Verse* (1909), *The Book of Restoration Verse* (1910), and *Our Lady's Choir: A Contemporary Anthology of Verse by Catholic Sisters* (1931). Though his stature as an eminent critic of American poetry continued to grow, Braithwaite never lost interest in British literature, which influenced his early writings. In 1919 he edited *The Book of Modern British Verse*, and in 1950 *The Bewitched Parsonage: The Story of the Brontës* appeared.

In 1935 Braithwaite, relinquishing his seat in Boston society, accepted the position of professor of creative literature at Atlanta University, where he remained for ten years. Despite his prestigious position in the world of letters, Braithwaite was painfully aware of his lack of formal education in the academic surroundings. It should not be surprising that he remained aloof from the politics of academia, never wavering in his devotion to his students. Braithwaite retired from Atlanta University in 1945 and moved to Harlem. His *Selected Poems* appeared in 1948, and he continued to write for various periodicals. He died on June 8, 1962.

◈ *Critical Extracts*

JOYCE KILMER   There are many beautiful poems in Mr. Braithwaite's collection ⟨*Anthology of Magazine Verse for 1913*⟩. Indeed, he includes a few poems that are not excellent. And he is wise enough to include poems widely different from each other in theme and spirit; to include, for instance, so classical and stately a composition as Sara Teasdale's splendid "Sappho," and so buoyant or rather boisterous a bit of enthusiasm as Nicholas Vachel Lindsay's "The Kallyope Yell." Mr. Braithwaite does not say, "Thus gods are made." He has taken the poet's point of view, as he says in the thoughtful essay which is his preface, and accepted his value of the theme he dealt with. And as a result his anthology contains poems differing widely in subject and style, but alike in the possession of sincerity and charm.

It is a gratifying commentary on American verse that so distinguished a collection can be made of one year's poetical output. Most readers will think of one or two poems which he would like to see added. ⟨. . .⟩ But no one will deny that the *Anthology of Magazine Verse for 1913* is a collection of real value; that its pages hold genuine poetry. Mr. Braithwaite has triumphantly refuted the charge that this is a prosaic land and a prosaic age.

Joyce Kilmer, "Last Year's Verse," *New York Times Review of Books*, 18 January 1914, p. 21

BENJAMIN BRAWLEY   Very recently (1917) Mr. Braithwaite has brought together in a volume, *The Poetic Year*, the series of articles which he contributed to the *Transcript* in 1916–17. The aim was in the form of conversations between a small group of friends to discuss the poetry of 1916. Says he: "There were four of us in the little group, and our common love for the art of poetry suggested a weekly meeting in the grove to discuss the books we had all agreed upon reading. . . . I made up my mind to record these discussions, and the setting as well, with all those other touches of human character and mood which never fail to enliven and give color to the serious business of art and life. . . . I gave fanciful names to my companions, Greek names which I am persuaded symbolized the spirit of each. There was nothing Psyche touched but made its soul apparent. Her wood-lore was beautiful and thorough; the very spirit of flowers, birds and trees was evoked when she went among them. Our other companion of her sex was Cassandra, and we gave her this name not because her forebodings were gloomy, but merely for her prophesying disposition, which was always building air-castles. The other member besides myself of our little group was Jason, of the heroic dreams and adventuresome spirit. He was restless in the bonds of a tranquillity that chafed the hidden spirit of his being." From the introduction we get something of the critic's own aims and ideals: "The conversational scheme of the book may, or may not, interest some readers. Poetry is a human thing, and it is time for the world—and especially our part of the world—to regard it as belonging to people. It sprang from the folk, and passed, when culture began to flourish, into the possession of a class. Now culture is passing from a class to the folk, and with it poetry is returning to its original possessors. It is in the spirit of these words that we discuss the poetry of the year." Emphasis is here given to this work because it is the sturdiest achievement of Mr. Braithwaite in the field in which he has recently become most distinguished, and even the brief quotations cited are sufficient to give some idea of his graceful, suggestive prose.

Benjamin Brawley, *The Negro in Literature and Art in the United States* (New York: Duffield, 1921), pp. 57–59

JAMES WELDON JOHNSON   Not many of the writers here included, except Dunbar, are known at all to the general reading public; and there is only one of these who has a widely recognized position in the American literary world, William Stanley Braithwaite. Mr. Braithwaite is not only unique in this respect, but he stands unique among all the Aframerican writers the United States has yet produced. He has gained his place, taking as the standard and measure for his work the identical standard and measure applied to American writers and American literature. He has asked for no allowances or rewards, either directly or indirectly, on account of his race.

Mr. Braithwaite is the author of two volumes of verses, lyrics of delicate and tenuous beauty. In his more recent and uncollected poems he shows himself more and more decidedly the mystic. But his place in American literature is due more to his place as a critic and anthologist than to his work as a poet. There is still another role he has played, that of friend of poetry and poets. It is a recognized fact that in the work which preceded the present revival of poetry in the United States, no one rendered more unremitting and valuable a service than Mr. Braithwaite. And it can be said that no future study of this age can be made without reference to Braithwaite.

> James Weldon Johnson, "Preface," *The Book of American Negro Poetry* (New York: Harcourt, Brace, & World, 1922), pp. 42–43

STERLING A. BROWN   In 1904, while Dunbar was alive, there appeared a volume of poems, *Lyrics of Life and Love*, and in 1907 another, *The House of Falling Leaves*, which equaled Dunbar's best work in finished artistry. These were the work of William Stanley Braithwaite who, through his criticisms and anthologies, was to become one of the pioneers in the poetry revival in America. Braithwaite was on terms of friendly intimacy with such important modern poets as Edwin Arlington Robinson and Amy Lowell, but the poetic qualities they sponsored or exemplified are not his. A widely read man, his poetry is derivative of the romantic tradition, the Pre-Raphaelites, and such poets of the end of the century as Swinburne and Ernest Dowson. It resembles what the French call "crepusculaire": poetry of the twilight. Favorite words are "dream" and "trance":

> Turn me to my yellow leaves,
> I am better satisfied. . . .
> Let me dream my dream entire
> Withered as an autumn leaf. . . .

Although he has written that the world to him is "a place of wonder" "just a will of God's to prove beauty" he reveals more of its wistful regret. "Death is life's best, truthful friend." An earlier mystical note

> This life we live so sensible and warm
> Is but a dreaming in a sleep that stays
> About us from the cradle to the grave—

becomes in later poems extremely obscure.

Braithwaite objected to his poems being classed indiscriminately as "Negro" poetry. A sensitive man of the library, he is concerned nowhere in his poems with race but wishes them to be "art for art's sake." The result is the usual one: the lines are graceful; at their best, exquisite, and not at their best, secondhand; but the substance is thin. Even the fugitive poetry of some of Braithwaite's masters had greater human sympathies.

Sterling A. Brown, *Negro Poetry and Drama* (Washington, DC: Associates in Negro Folk Education, 1937), pp. 49–50

J. SAUNDERS REDDING   Various explanations have been given for the oddity which a study of certain Negro poets like Braithwaite presents, but not one of them takes into account the pressure of the age. It is not considered that the expression of certain thoughts, feelings, and ideas was denied if they wished the hearing of an important audience. No one of the explanations mentions that all but one of these poets wrote better verse on material that in the very nature of things was (rather than is) Negro material. Braithwaite is the exception. On this general head, Countee Cullen has something to say in the preface to *Caroling Dusk:* "Since theirs [Negro writers] is also the heritage of the English language, their work will not present any serious aberration from the poetic tendencies of their time . . . for the double obligation of being both Negro and American is not so unified as we are often led to believe." Also, and apparently by way of explanation, Braithwaite's autobiographical sketch has this to say: "I inherited the incentives and ideals of the intellect from an ancestry of British gentlemen." Further, it might be pointed out that he was born in Boston and has lived most of his life in Massachusetts. These remarks are definitely offered in the nature of excuses for divergence from the racial norm of creative ends.

J. Saunders Redding, *To Make a Poet Black* (Chapel Hill: University of North Carolina Press, 1939), pp. 89–90

DAVID DAICHES   Mr. Braithwaite writes—and for some time has been writing—what is usually called "traditional poetry," or, as the publishers put it, "in the classical tradition" (by which they apparently mean the tradition of nineteenth-century romantic poetry). He is not, however, a mere dabbler in Victorian echoes, though he does for the most part employ the imagery and the diction of Victorian poetry. His poetry is filled with individual perceptions of man and nature, speculations on history and morality, moods and introspections. He is at his best when introspective, for here the nineteenth-century idiom seems somehow to fit his insights. When he tries to become memorial or lapidary his style can reach the absurdity of: "Against this wrong of Teutonic might / From lease-lend stores we give the Nations aid / Who stand embattled, but are unafraid." Even at his best, however, he gives us nothing of which we can not find better prototypes elsewhere and though Mr. Braithwaite is to be congratulated on his success in working within a nineteenth-century idiom and his refusal to be seduced by any poet later than Housman, one cannot help wondering whether it is all worth it.

> David Daiches, "In Nineteenth-Century Idiom," *New York Herald Tribune Weekly Book Review*, 6 February 1949, p. 12

PHILIP BUTCHER   Recalling his years as a member of the English faculty at Atlanta University, William Stanley Braithwaite thought some of his colleagues "rather offish" and quite degree conscious.

> Always in an institution of that sort your colleagues are interested to know where you got your education and where you got your degrees, and I told them frankly I had no earned degrees, not even a high school diploma. I don't know just what they thought, but sometimes their action was a puzzlement. They had a conference there of English teachers from Negro colleges. I'm not much for conferences. The man who was the head of the English Department at Morehouse College, Nathaniel P. Tillman, invited me to become a member, and I said, "I don't want to become a member."

⟨. . .⟩ He said that once he refused the command of his department chairman that he attend a staff meeting to prepare an examination on the fundamentals, reminding her that he had come to the university in 1935 to teach literature to English majors and to direct the research of graduate students. He was not insensitive to the plight of students who had cultural deprivation; he had a strong commitment to and rapport with those youths who heard his occasional chapel lectures as well as with the select few who were enrolled in his advanced courses. But he felt the need to reserve his energies for the specific tasks he had undertaken. And he had a sense of special vulnerability as an intruder from the non-academic world, unsupported by the conventional credentials of the profession. During his early months on the faculty he could not quite understand what seemed to him a lack of cordiality, and it was not until a year or two had passed that he learned the aloofness he detected was due to his colleagues' respect for his status in the world of letters rather than to scorn for the inadequacies of his formal training.

He was "Dr. Braithwaite" on campus by virtue of an honorary Doctor of Literature degree granted by Talladega College in 1918; Atlanta had given him an honorary M.A. in the same year. As testimonials to his learning these awards were superfluous. Though his poetry seems now of minor significance, his attainments as critic, editor, and anthologist add up to genuine distinction. Since 1906 his reviews and articles in the Boston *Transcript* had made him a literary figure of national importance, one of the best informed and most influential critics of poetry in America. His period anthologies of English poetry, beginning with *The Book of Elizabethan Verse* in 1906, and the seventeen annual collections of the best American magazine verse he compiled until the Depression put an end to the series were standards of their kind. As president of the B. J. Brimmer Company he published such works as the first novel of James Gould Cozzens and Georgia Douglas Johnson's *Bronze*. His extraordinarily wide acquaintance with poets, editors, novelists, publishers, and literary notables of all sorts is attested by the hundreds of pieces of correspondence in the Braithwaite Papers that Harvard University acquired for its library at Depression rates. If Braithwaite was short on academic credentials, there was no question whatever about his real qualifications as a teacher. Nor was there doubt about his devotion to the youngsters he exerted himself to know both as students and people. To them, to his colleagues, and to skeptical administrators he reiterated one conviction: a lack of background—of formal educational training or personal cultural advantages—need not prevent intellectual or artistic achievement. He had his own career as irrefutable evidence of the validity of his doctrine.

> Philip Butcher, "William Stanley Braithwaite and the College Language Association," *CLA Journal* 15, No. 2 (December 1971): 117–20

PHILIP BUTCHER   Writing in praise of William Stanley Braithwaite, awarded the 1918 Spingarn Medal as "the American citizen of African descent who made last year the highest achievement in any field of elevated human endeavor," W. E. B. Du Bois called him "the most prominent critic of poetry in America." So influential was Braithwaite at the time that a celebrated rival, Harriet Monroe, dubbed him "Sir Oracle" and "the Boston dictator." Poets as notable as Robert Frost and Amy Lowell courted his favor, as did Claude McKay and Countee Cullen. William Dean Howells, who spoke with the highest authority, once said Braithwaite was "the most intellectual historian of contemporary poetry I know." Yet this poet, critic, editor, anthologist, and publisher, whose books fill a whole shelf, has been ignored or slighted in most textbooks and histories of American literature as a whole, and even in the current flood of anthologies and studies of "the black experience" he has received less recognition than his labors and accomplishments merit. ⟨. . .⟩

On February 14, 1906, Braithwaite began to contribute to the Boston *Evening Transcript*, a newspaper that enjoyed at that time a status not unlike that of today's *New York Times*. The reviews and essays he published in its pages were a major source of income for him for twenty years, though he was never a salaried staff member. They constituted the bulk of his critical writing and the principal basis for his authority in the world of letters. Through them, he labored to enlarge the audience for verse, encourage and assist fledgling poets, and win for talent and genius appropriate recognition. He became a significant force in revitalizing poetry in America.

One outgrowth of his work with the *Transcript* was his publication of a slender *Anthology of Magazine Verse for 1913*. For the next sixteen years he issued his annual selection of the best poetry printed in the nation's periodicals. Braithwaite exhibited a wide range of taste, conscientious objectivity, and a fine capacity for exhibiting poetry that would endure. His personal predilection for the Pre-Raphaelites and late romantics did not affect his appreciation for other kinds of poetry. (His own verse, much overshadowed in importance by his other writings, has a richer variety than is supposed; though he wrote often in the manner of Ernest Dowson, his model was sometimes Edwin Arlington Robinson, Marianne Moore, or even Dylan Thomas.) Conservative critical pronouncements in the *Transcript* and elsewhere did nothing to enhance his influence once conservative tenets ceased to be the rule in American poetry. And the very pursuits that brought him prestige doomed him to a diminishing stature. No one engaged in writing appreciative newspaper essays on poets for a livelihood could help but be unduly generous in the long run, and no annual selection of the "best" verse, largely dependent for survival on the commercial support of poets themselves, could hold to rigid standards of excellence and a careful discrimination.

Yet poets regarded an invitation to reprint their lines in "Braithwaite" as tantamount to an award of merit; scholars still find the bibliographies and other editorial paraphernalia of these volumes valuable to their studies; and bibliophiles treasure the books because they first acclaimed poets that are now accepted as minor classics. Especially demonstrative of Braithwaite's discernment is the 1915 anthology which included E. A. Robinson's "Flammonde," Amy Lowell's "Patterns," Wallace Stevens's "Peter Quince at the Clavier," and Robert Frost's "Birches," "The Road Not Taken," and "The Death of a Hired Man." That volume also offered a poem by James Weldon Johnson, and black poets were represented in the later annuals in increasing numbers. As Margaret Haley Carpenter has said, no other annual collections of poetry "commanded the literary excitement, the prestige, or the popularity accorded these volumes." Both Braithwaite's position and disposition encouraged a wide acquaintance among aspiring and established poets; the Index of Names for correspondence in the William Stanley Braithwaite Papers at Harvard University runs to more than thirteen typed pages, single-spaced and double column. His reputation as discoverer and mentor of new talent is thoroughly deserved.

> Philip Butcher, "Introduction," *The William Stanley Braithwaite Reader* (Ann Arbor: University of Michigan Press, 1972), pp. 1, 3–4

LOUIS D. RUBIN, JR.   Braithwaite's refusal to use the condition of the black man as subject matter for his poetry (in his critical prose he dealt with it much more directly) drew the fire of militant critics as constituting an attempt to deny his own identity and to avoid his responsibility as a black man in a society that discriminated against black men. From the standpoint of literary criticism, the test must be more pragmatic: the critic must look at Braithwaite's poems, and ask whether this decision to avoid all racial identity had a deleterious effect on what he wrote. The problem is a complex one; it involves, by implication at least, the whole question of the relationship of literature and society, and of the nature and sources of artistic creativity. When we examine Braithwaite's poetry, what seems most striking is its combination of technical sophistication and thinness of feeling. It is a poetry of surfaces—dextrous and finely wrought, but lacking in human significance. Few of Braithwaite's fellow black poets could produce lyrics as technically perfect as his "Del Cascar," with the subtle rhythms of its last stanza:

> The sun went down through crimson bars,
> And left his blind face battered with stars,
> But the brown toes of China kept
> Hot the tears Del Cascar wept!

Yet it is a technique in a vacuum; "Del Cascar," like most of Braithwaite's poetry, settles for a surface, offering for its meaning only a faint tinge of melancholy. Even his "autobiographical" sequence, "Sandy Star," leaves the reader with only a sense of wry wistfulness and incompleteness. The truth would seem to be that Braithwaite's refusal as a poet to deal directly with his social identity is emblematic of a refusal in his poetry to confront any but the obvious aspects of his own individuality. In suppressing his blackness, he suppressed his human uniqueness, producing a poetry of surface effects, deficient in importance both for society and self. What is missing is not so much the specific personality of a black man, as any personality at all.

Louis D. Rubin, Jr., "The Search for a Language, 1746–1923," *Black Poetry in America: Two Essays in Historical Interpretation* by Blyden Jackson and Louis D. Rubin, Jr. (Baton Rouge: Louisiana State University Press, 1974), pp. 31–32

KENNY J. WILLIAMS   By 1929 Braithwaite was surveying annually over 200 magazines and newspapers. Despite the range and diversity of his sources, however, his anthologies of course only approximate inclusiveness. Still, he generally succeeds in selecting from each year's offering the best and most representative pieces. "Objective" even though personally and artistically conservative (just as ⟨Harriet⟩ Monroe was conservative), adamant that all poetic views and voices be heard, Braithwaite supported not only the Imagist movement but those younger poets who had succumbed neither to eastern traditions nor to academic conceptions of verse. Among this latter group were the bohemians and experimenters whose intensity and vitality energized American literature. Braithwaite's attentions—consistently prophetic—thrust forward avant garde writers who otherwise may have suffered neglect. ⟨. . .⟩

Monroe deals most specifically with women poets in *Poets and Their Art;* Braithwaite, however, devotes a number of years to the issue of Afro-American art, his views on it shaped and determined by his evolving aesthetic principles. Despite his apparent equivocation on racial matters, he did much to make the work of the Harlem Renaissance more accessible to the general American reading public. Yet the excesses of the movement, and especially the poetry of Claude McKay, disturbed this genteel man. Certainly, McKay's power lies partially in his own ability to embody an altered sonnet from sincere protests against an emasculating and dehumanizing system—"If We Must Die" is a case in point. But for Braithwaite the province of poetry excludes such protest, and if as a lyricist he recognizes McKay's innovative treatment of the sonnet tradition, as a critic he condemns him—in "The Negro in Literature," from the September 1924 issue of *The Crisis*—as a "violent and angry propagandist" who uses "his natural poetic gifts" to voice "defiant thoughts." We cannot know today the extent to which Braithwaite's antipathy was predicated on McKay's radical political associations, or his violation—in Braithwaite's view—of an "art-for-art's-sake" principle. Yet that he supported aesthetically motivated "Negro poetry" is clear; indeed, in essays appearing in such publications as *Colored American Magazine, The Crisis*, and *Opportunity*, Braithwaite contributes to the developing black aesthetic.

Of course, Braithwaite occasionally evinces the gentility made famous by his Boston literary circle. In his review of Jessie Fauset, for instance, he claims her novels of the middle class to be excellent studies and Fauset herself to be among the outstanding female novelists in America. In fact, he goes so far as to call her "the Jane Austen of Negro Literature."

Overt literary protest annoyed Braithwaite's sensibilities, but neither did he respect those writers who—in catering to the whimsy of white audiences—denigrate themselves. He was one of the first American critics to perceive that Paul Laurence Dunbar had ended one era of Afro-American literature and, for better or for worse, initiated another. As against Howells's claim that Dunbar represents "the soul" of his people, Braithwaite felt that he merely interprets "a folk temperament." (That neither critic pays much attention to Dunbar's standard English verse is probably not suprising.) Braithwaite rejected as well the double standard of critics and artists who insisted on the innately exotic and primitive nature of Afro-American literature. Nor could he tolerate white writers who falsified black portraits. Such racist novelists as Thomas Dixon, he argues, move "from caricature to libel"; and even the sympathetic Eugene O'Neill is unable to perceive "the immense paradox of racial life."

In an age not known for sophisticated racial advancements, Braithwaite did bridge one gap, at least, between the black and white worlds: his long association with the Boston *Evening Transcript* is ample evidence of his acceptance among the Boston Brahmins. As early as 1906, the Boston

Author's Club elected him to membership, and among his close friends he counted such New Englanders as Thomas Wentworth Higginson, Julia Ward Howe, Thomas Bailey Aldrich, Bliss Perry, and Edward Everett Hale. In 1907, too, he accepted an invitation to participate in the centenary celebration of John Greenleaf Whittier's birth, for which occasion he wrote the ode "White Magic," a comparison of social and aesthetic literary modes.

⟨. . .⟩ If one can accept Braithwaite's belief that a commitment to the totality of American experience does not invalidate a specific cultural or racial heritage—if one can accept the diversity of Afro-American literature itself, and assume that *blackness* and *whiteness* need not be in themselves determining aesthetic criteria—then Braithwaite, who deserves to be remembered, ceases to be a literary phenomenon.

> Kenny J. Williams, "An Invisible Partnership and Unlikely Relationship: William Stanley Braithwaite and Harriet Monroe," *Callaloo* 10, No. 3 (Summer 1987): 548–50

▦ *Bibliography*

Lyrics of Life and Love. 1904.

The Book of Elizabethan Verse (editor). 1906.

The House of Falling Leaves, with Other Poems. 1908.

The Book of Georgian Verse (editor). 1909.

The Book of Restoration Verse (editor). 1910.

The Poetry of Thomas S. Jones, Jr. (with Jessie B. Rittenhouse and Edward J. O'Brien). 1910.

Anthology of Magazine Verse for 1913 (editor). 1913.

Anthology of Magazine Verse for 1914 (editor). 1914.

Anthology of Magazine Verse for 1915 (editor). 1915.

Representative American Poetry (editor; with Henry Thomas Schittkind). 1916.

Anthology of Magazine Verse for 1916 and Year Book of American Poetry (editor). 1916.

The Poetic Year for 1916: A Critical Anthology (editor). 1917.

Anthology of Magazine Verse for 1917 and Year Book of American Poetry (editor). 1917.

The Golden Treasury of Magazine Verse (editor). 1918.

Anthology of Magazine Verse for 1918 and Year Book of American Poetry (editor). 1918.

Victory! Celebrated by Thirty-eight American Poets (editor). 1919.

The Story of the Great War. 1919.

Anthology of Magazine Verse for 1919 and Year Book of American Poetry (editor). 1919.

The Book of Modern British Verse (editor). 1919.

Anthology of Magazine Verse for 1920 and Year Book of American Poetry (editor). 1920.

Anthology of Magazine Verse for 1921 and Year Book of American Poetry (editor). 1921.

Anthology of Massachusetts Poets (editor). 1922.

Anthology of Magazine Verse for 1922 and Yearbook of American Poetry (editor). 1922.

Anthology of Magazine Verse for 1923 and Yearbook of American Poetry (editor). 1923.

Anthology of Magazine Verse for 1924 and Yearbook of American Poetry (editor). 1924.

Anthology of Magazine Verse for 1925 and Yearbook of American Poetry (editor). 1925.

Anthology of Magazine Verse for 1926 and Yearbook of American Poetry (editor). 1926.

John Myers O'Hara and the Grecian Influence. 1926.

Anthology of Magazine Verse for 1927 and Yearbook of American Poetry (editor). 1927.

Anthology of Magazine Verse for 1928 and Yearbook of American Poetry (editor). 1928.

Anthology of Magazine Verse for 1929 and Yearbook of American Poetry (editor). 1929.

Our Lady's Choir: A Contemporary Anthology of Verse by Catholic Sisters (editor). 1931.

Selected Poems. 1948.

The Bewitched Parsonage: The Story of the Brontës. 1950.

Anthology of Magazine Verse for 1958; and Anthology of Poems from the Seventeen Previously Published Braithwaite Anthologies (editor; with Margaret Haley Carpenter). 1959.

The William Stanley Braithwaite Reader. Ed. Philip Butcher. 1972.

William Wells Brown
c. 1814–1884

WILLIAM WELLS BROWN was born outside Lexington, Kentucky, around 1814 to a slave named Elizabeth. He was one of seven children of Elizabeth, each of whom had a different father. It is likely that Brown's father was the half-brother of John Young, his master, although Brown was never certain of his paternity. In 1827 Brown and his family were moved to a farm north of St. Louis. Brown showed his intelligence even as a child and, instead of being sent to the fields, was hired out for work in the city. Brown's work as a printer's helper for the *St. Louis Times* and as a physician's assistant to Dr. Young provided a short reprieve from the usual trials of slavery and stimulated Brown's intellect. Later, however, Brown was hired to a slave trader, James Walker, for whom he tended slaves bound for sale in Natchez or New Orleans. This task was made more painful when he learned that his family was being sold and separated. In 1833, after Brown failed in an escape attempt with his mother, she was sold south, never to be seen again, and Brown was sold to Enoch Price.

Price proved to be Brown's last master, for on New Year's Day, 1834, Brown escaped and undertook an arduous journey to freedom. Along the road, after much hardship, he was taken in and nursed by a Quaker from whom he took his surname. Now free, Brown worked diligently to start a new life and in 1834 married Elizabeth Schooner, with whom he had three daughters. He was quickly drawn to the abolitionists and provided a link in the Underground Railroad, ferrying escaped slaves to Canada. Much affected by the speeches of Frederick Douglass, Brown also began to lecture. After unleashing his powerful and often humorous tongue, he was embraced by William Lloyd Garrison's wing of the abolitionist movement and the American Anti-Slavery Society and published many essays in abolitionist papers. Brown's lecturing schedule was relentless, but he was determined to reach an even greater audience; in 1847 he published *Narrative of William W. Brown, a Fugitive Slave*, which became a best-selling antislavery work. The *Narrative* showed Brown to be highly skilled in the use of dialogue, anecdote, and argument, while powerfully retelling the dramatic scenes common to slavery and slave narratives.

In 1849 Brown, recently elected to the World Peace Congress, traveled to Europe on a lecture tour. His sojourn was turned into an exile with the passage of the Fugitive Slave Act in 1850, which prevented him from returning to the free states. Brown undertook an exhausting series of lectures in Europe for the next five years, meeting many celebrities of the day. In 1852 he published *Three Years in Europe*, a travel book; a year later appeared *Clotel; or, The President's Daughter*, the first novel to be published by a black American. This complex novel, full of plots and subplots, is a fictional account of the life of a mulatto woman rumored to be the illegitimate child of Thomas Jefferson and one of his slaves. Though the novel is occasionally fantastic in plot, Brown's use of excerpts from legal codes and religious sermons, his descriptions of slave auctions, hunts, and lynchings, and his rich portrayal of the slave mentality give it an authoritative, and sometimes epic, tone. In 1854 Brown's British friends purchased his freedom and he returned to the United States, where he published three revisions of *Clotel*: *Miralda; or, The Beautiful Quadroon* (serialized 1860–61); *Clotelle: A Tale of the Southern States* (1864); and *Clotelle; or, The Colored Heroine* (1867).

Brown also published a number of other works showing his versatility as a writer. Among these was *The Escape; or, A Leap for Freedom* (1858), the first play to be published by a black American writer. Brown wrote other dramas, but they do not appear to survive. Other works include *St. Domingo: Its Revolutions and Its Patriots*, a historical work; *The American Fugitive in Europe* (1855), an enlargement of his travel book; a *Memoir* (1859); and *The Black Man, His Antecedents, His Genius, and His Achievements* (1863), a chronicle of the historical importance of African civilizations and contemporary black Americans.

After the Civil War Brown, like many abolitionists, continued to lecture about the plight of the newly freed slaves, as well as other issues of civil rights, such as women's suffrage. His three final books focus on the historical role of black Americans: *The Negro in the American Rebellion: His Heroism and His Fidelity* (1867); *The Rising Son* (1873); and *My Southern Home* (1880). Brown died on November 6, 1884, and was buried in Cambridge, Massachusetts, in an unmarked grave.

◈ *Critical Extracts*

JOSEPHINE BROWN   This pretended fastidiousness on the part of the whites has produced some of the most ridiculous scenes. William Wells Brown, while travelling through Ohio in 1844, went from Sandusky to Republic, on the Mad River and Lake Erie Railroad. On arriving at Sandusky, he learned that colored people were not allowed to take seats in the cars with whites, and that, as there was no *Jim Crow car* on that road, blacks were generally made to ride in the baggage-car. Mr. Brown, however, went into one of the best passenger cars, seated himself, crossed his legs, and looked as unconcerned as if the car had been made for his sole use. At length, one of the railway officials entered the car, and asked him what he was doing there. "I am going to Republic," said Mr. Brown. "You can't ride here," said the conductor. "Yes I can," returned the colored man. "No you can't," rejoined the railway man. "Why?" inquired Mr. Brown. "Because we don't allow *niggers* to ride with white people," replied the conductor. "Well I shall remain here," said Mr. Brown. "You will see, pretty soon, whether you will or not," retorted the railway man, as he turned to leave the car. By this time, the passengers were filling up the seats, and every thing being made ready to start. After an absence of a few minutes, the conductor again entered the car, accompanied by two stout men, and took Mr. Brown by the collar and pulled him out. Pressing business demanded that Mr. Brown should go, and by that train; he therefore got into the freight car, just as the train was moving off. Seating himself on a flour barrel, he took from his pocket the last number of the *Liberator,* and began reading it. On went the train, making its usual stops, until within four or five miles of Republic, when the conductor, (who, by-the-by, was the same man who had moved Mr. Brown from the passenger car) demanded his ticket. "I have no ticket," returned he. "Then I will take your fare," said the conductor. "How much is it?" inquired Mr. Brown. "One dollar and a quarter," was the answer. "How much do you charge those who ride in the passenger cars?" inquired the colored man. "The same," said the conductor. "Do you suppose that I will pay the same price for riding up here in the freight car, that those do who are in the passenger car?" asked Mr. Brown. "Certainly," replied the conductor. "Well, you are very much mistaken, if you think any such thing," said the passenger. "Come, black man, out with your money, and none of your nonsense with me," said the conductor. "I won't pay you the price you demand, and that's the end of it," said Mr. Brown. "Don't you intend paying your fare?" inquired the conductor. "Yes," replied the colored man; "but I won't pay you a dollar and a quarter." "What do you intend to pay, then?" demanded the official. "I will pay what's right, but I don't intend to give you all that sum." "Well, then," said the conductor, "as you have had to ride in the freight car, give me one dollar and you may go." "I won't do any such thing," returned Mr. Brown. "Why won't you?" inquired the railway man. "If I had come in the passenger car, I would have paid as much as others do; but I won't ride up here on a flour barrel, and pay you a dollar." "You think yourself as good as white people, I suppose?" said the conductor; and his eyes flashed as if he meant what he said. "Well, being you seem to feel so bad because you had to ride in the freight car, give me seventy-five cents, and I'll say no more about it," continued he. "No, I won't. If I had been permitted to ride with the other passengers, I would pay what you first demanded; but I won't pay seventy-five cents for riding up here, astride a flour barrel, in the hot sun." "Don't you intend paying at all?" asked the conductor. "Yes, I will pay what is right." "Give me half a dollar, and I will say no more about it." "No, I won't," returned the other; "I shall not pay fifty cents for riding in a freight car." "What will you pay, then?" demanded the conductor. "What do you charge per hundred on this road?" asked Mr. Brown. "Twenty-five cents," answered the conductor. "Then I will pay you thirty-seven and a half cents," said the passenger, "for I weigh just one hundred and fifty pounds." "Do you expect to get off by paying that trifling sum?" "I have come as freight, and I will pay for freight, and nothing more," said Mr. Brown. The conductor took the thirty-seven and a half cents, declaring, as he left the car, that that was the most impudent negro that ever travelled on that road.

Josephine Brown, *Biography of an American Bondman, By His Daughter* (1856), *Two Biographies by African-American Women* (New York: Oxford University Press, 1991), pp. 56–59

VERNON LOGGINS   From 1854 to 1863 Brown is regularly referred to in the antislavery papers as engaged for lectures. During this most active period of his career as an abolitionist agent, he possibly took the time to make a trip to the West Indies, and he is credited with having written during this period a second novel, *Miralda, or, The Beautiful Quadroon.* But if such a work was ever printed, it seems to be no longer in existence. This is likewise true of *Doughface*, a drama, which has been attributed to Brown and which might possibly have been written before 1858. But since we cannot prove that *Doughface* ever existed, we must take

Brown's *The Escape; or, A Leap for Freedom*, published in 1858, as the American Negro's first definitely known attempt to write a play.

Brown claimed that he wrote *The Escape* for his "own amusement." He said:

> I read it privately, however, to a circle of friends, and through them was invited to read it before a Literary Society. Since then the Drama has been given in various parts of the country.

He meant, of course, that he had given it as a reading; and it seems that the public for a time preferred it to his lectures. The play is made up of five acts, each divided into many scenes. Some of the farcical episodes are diverting, but the attempts at seriousness are unpardonably forced. The slave heroine, Melinda, pours out freely such sentiments as the following, which she speaks to her amorous master after he has lured her to a hut on one of his remote plantations:

> Sir, I am your slave; you can do what you please with the avails of my labor, but you shall never tempt me to swerve from the path of virtue.

Her husband, Glen, also a slave, indulges in endless antislavery heroics. One does not wonder that it is good luck rather than the initiative of the two which in the end lands them safe in Canada. *The Escape* as a play is far more feeble than *Clotel* is as a novel. However, since *The Escape* is a pioneer venture of the American Negro into the field of the drama, it is a landmark in his literature.

Vernon Loggins, *The Negro Author: His Development in America* (New York: Columbia University Press, 1931), pp. 168–69

W. EDWARD FARRISON   It was reported in *The Liberator* for April 25 that Brown had written "a very interesting drama" with the Reverend Dr. Adams as its protagonist, that he had read it "to great acceptance in some of the surrounding towns," and that he intended to read it in Boston "during Anniversary week"—the last week in May, during which the Annual New England Anti-Slavery Convention was usually held. The report in *The Liberator* also quoted the one in the Worcester *Daily Spy* for April 12.

This satirical work was eventually entitled *Experience, Or How to Give a Northern Man a Backbone*. It is not improbable, however, that Brown at first gave it another title by which it might have been occasionally identified long afterwards. In his *Men of Mark: Eminent, Progressive and Rising* (Cleveland, Ohio, 1887), I, 449, William J. Simmons credited Brown with writing a drama entitled *Doe Face*—thus Simmons spelled the title. I have found no instance in which Brown referred to any work of his by the title *Doughface*, but this shorter less descriptive title is more or less applicable to *Experience*. Nor have I found any references by Brown to but one other drama written by himself, namely, *The Escape; or, A Leap for Freedom*; and the title *Doughface* could never have been considered suitable for that work. It may well be, therefore, that the title mentioned by Simmons was the first one by which *Experience* was known. I know of no reason for supposing that Brown ever published this play, but he frequently presented it as a dramatic reading during the next year, even after he had written another and perhaps better play.

Brown had read a considerable number of plays, including many of Shakespeare's, and he had seen some of the latter as well as many others on the stage in both America and Great Britain. Accordingly, whether he had any noteworthy genius or none for writing plays, he was not ignorant of the exigencies of the stage. His plot, it may be observed, was compact and full of dramatic situations—experiences by which a doughface doctor of divinity was reformed into an abolitionist.

Experience consisted of three acts divided respectively into two, five, and two scenes, the last of which ended with a "Grand Poetical Finale." In the first scene the playwright gave himself an excellent opportunity to let Adderson reveal himself in a Faustian or Richard-the-Third soliloquy. In Act II there were the quirkish circumstances under which Adderson was kidnapped and sold into slavery—a business in which the landlord of a hotel in Richmond, Virginia, and a slave-trader presumably colluded; there was the breaking of the new and apparently recalcitrant white slave; there were the more or less farcical situations in which Adderson and the slaves Dinah and Sam were involved; there was the climactic scene in which Adderson repented for formerly condoning slavery and avowed his hatred of it. Finally there was the scene in Adderson's home in Boston, after his release from slavery and return home, in which Marcus, a fugitive slave, arrived at an opportune time and spoke so eloquently of human freedom that Adderson resolved to help him to achieve it in Canada. The erstwhile doughface had at last become possessed of a backbone as well as a conscience.

W. Edward Farrison, "Brown's First Drama," *CLA Journal* 2, No. 2 (December 1958): 105–6

us the influences of his work, but will form for us as well the rock mountain base from which he finally soared as a creative artist. This understanding of both background and foreground will mark our complete portrait of the artist.

> J. Noel Heermance, *William Wells Brown and* Clotelle: *A Portrait of the Artist in the First Negro Novel* (Hamden, CT: Archon Books, 1969), pp. 22–23

BLYDEN JACKSON   ⟨. . .⟩ Brown's main function as a working abolitionist was to lecture. It has been said that in England alone, during his five years of residence there, he made a thousand speeches. "The great weakness of *Clotel*," according to Vernon Loggins, "is that enough material for a dozen novels is crowded into its two-hundred and forty-five pages." Loggins' observation may well utter its own indictment of *Clotel*. Yet it may be even more perceptive, apropos of *Clotel*, to say of it that what fills its pages is not so much a dozen novels as a dozen, or more, abolitionist lectures. For it is the art of rhetoric, rather than the disciplines of inspired narration, which seems to determine the organization and the style, in addition to the content, of *Clotel*. The novel is an abolitionist *tour de force* not only in its borrowings of subject matter. It is a succession of abolitionist diatribes in the method of its presentation. As it is episodic, it is also a progression, or really a somewhat frenzied scramble, from one *exemplum* in an abolitionist homily to another. And if Brown never creates engaging characters in *Clotel*, and never surrounds his stiffly moving marionettes there with a world that comes alive, it may easily be because he was not able to shed, even in a novel, the habits of thought and modes of literary creativity he had accustomed himself to use on an abolitionist's lecturer's platform. ⟨. . .⟩

As a work of thought (and of practical use), *Clotel* may be explored with fair rewards. The student of the Negro novel can and should, for example, conclude that Clotel herself, a stipulated quadroon, embodies the theme of the tragic mulatto, a prominent theme-to-be in the Negro novel until, and even through, the Harlem Renaissance of the 1920s. He may note that Currer, Clotel's mother, who never legally marries, is yet a matriarch, and that *Clotel*, in which men play only secondary roles, is a history of a matriarchate, except for the marriage of one of Currer's daughters to a white man in New Orleans. Thus *Clotel* may be linked, by thought, to the sociology which has expatiated at length upon matriarchy and the Negro. *Clotel* lingers in, and around, Natchez. It is there that Peck, a northerner come South, resides. Brown uses Peck to illustrate the abasement of organized religion when it capitulates to slavery. He also uses Peck the northerner to suggest the economic interest which, in northerners, could, and often did, lead them to sell their souls, in effect, to slavery. Within the penumbra of implication surrounding Peck may be readily discerned, in a reflective analysis, a train of northern shipmasters, northern millowners, northern merchants, northern bankers, and northern moneylenders. But none of the northerners in this train are really shipmasters, millowners, merchants, bankers, or moneylenders. None of them, that is, are properly imagined for a tale of fiction. All of them, if they are seen in any way, appear only because the mind, catching hold of an idea, seizes upon them as pieces that fit in to help make this idea whole. They are noumena, works of thought, and thus only of practical use. But they should be, as should be Clotel, more than that. Shadowy or not, they should approach us as through a living dream. And Clotel, of course, especially in a novel which is named after her, after a *person*, should cross that magic boundary a transcendence of which would place her beside the convincing characters of the great Victorians. That she does not, simplistic as it may be, is a measure—indeed, the measure above all other measures—of *Clotel*'s failure.

The year before the year in which *Clotel* appeared had introduced the sweeping triumph of *Uncle Tom's Cabin*. Brown knew, of course, of *Uncle Tom's Cabin*. There is no reason to doubt but that its success encouraged him. He could, in 1853, not only calculate on finding occupation for his relatively idle moments by producing *Clotel*. He could, if he was in an exhilarated mood, hitch, at least in dreams, his wagon to a best seller's star. He could, that is, daydream of writing another *Uncle Tom's Cabin*. And he could daydream, moreover, of writing it, not merely for his own financial gain, but also for the greater glory of the antislavery cause. Whatever his aspirations and motives, however, whatever his dreams and hopes—they all foundered. *Clotel* did not become another *Uncle Tom's Cabin*. Nor has Clotel ever become another Uncle Tom. She is not, and never was, a household word. Neither is the even more idealized Clotelle. Yet they are what we have, all we have, however they may be limited and bereft, of the first protagonist in a Negro novel. They establish a point of departure. And knowledge of them, whatever their condition and their goods or evils, is indispensable in a full history of the Negro novel.

Blyden Jackson, A *History of Afro-American Literature* (Baton Rouge: Louisiana State University Press, 1989), Vol. 1, pp. 339–42.

▧ *Bibliography*

Narrative of William W. Brown, a Fugitive Slave, Written by Himself. 1847, 1848.

A Lecture Delivered Before the Female Anti-Slavery Society of Salem, at Lyceum Hall, Nov. 14, 1847. 1847.

The Anti-Slavery Harp: A Collection of Songs for Anti-Slavery Meetings (editor). 1848.

A Description of William Wells Brown's Original Panoramic Views of the Scenes in the Life of an American Slave. 1849.

Three Years in Europe; or, Places I Have Seen and People I Have Met. 1852, 1855 (as *The American Fugitive in Europe: Sketches of Places and People Abroad*).

Clotel; or, The President's Daughter: A Narrative of Slave Life in the United States. 1853, 1861 (as *Miralda; or, The Beautiful Quadroon: A Romance of American Slavery, Founded on Fact*), 1864 (as *Clotelle: A Tale of the Southern States*), 1867 (as *Clotelle; or, The Colored Heroine*).

St. Domingo: Its Revolutions and Its Patriots. 1855.

The Escape; or, A Leap for Freedom. 1858.

Memoir of William Wells Brown, an American Bondman: Written by Himself. 1859.

The Black Man, His Antecedents, His Genius, and His Achievements. 1863.

The Negro in the American Rebellion: His Heroism and His Fidelity. 1867.

The Rising Son; or, The Antecedents and Advancement of the Colored Race. 1873.

My Southern Home; or, The South and Its People. 1880.

Joseph Seamon Cotter, Sr.
1861–1949

JOSEPH SEAMON COTTER, SR. was born on February 2, 1861, near Bardstown, Kentucky. His father, Micheil J. Cotter, was a sixty-year-old educated white man; his mother, Martha Vaughn, was a freeborn black woman of mixed African, English, and Cherokee heritage and was working for the Cotters as a nurse when she became pregnant. Martha Vaughn moved to Louisville with her son when he was four months old. Although, because of financial difficulties, Cotter's formal education ended when he was eight, his mother had a great love of books and taught Cotter herself. Cotter reportedly got an early start as a writer, creating stories so that the boys and men of the brickyard in which he worked would like him.

Cotter worked in a variety of menial positions until he was twenty-two years old. At that time he met Louisville educator William T. Peyton, who convinced Cotter to give up his latest job (prizefighting) and attend school. Cotter became qualified to teach, and, beginning in 1885, taught at private and public schools in and around Louisville. In 1891 Cotter married Maria F. Cox, a former school principal, and had three children, all of whom died young. His second child, Joseph, Jr., began a career as a poet before dying of tuberculosis at the age of twenty-three.

Cotter published his first collection of poetry, A Rhyming, in 1895, followed by Links of Friendship in 1898. Although initially his works consciously imitated traditional English poetry in both form and content, his later poetry is more contemporary, more topical, and more regional. In 1903 Cotter published Caleb, the Degenerate, a four-act blank verse play espousing Booker T. Washington's philosophy of practical agricultural and industrial training as the surest means of social uplift for black Americans. Cotter continued to explore racial themes in his 1909 collection of poetry A White Song and a Black One. This collection is divided into halves: the first half ("A White Song") is a general treatment of Southern attitudes, society, and history, and the second half ("A Black Song") contains a number of dialect poems and describes black life in the South. In 1912 Cotter published his only collection of short fiction, *Negro Tales*.

More than twenty years passed before Cotter published again. At that time he edited a commemorative book about the black community that he organized and in which he lived, entitled *Twenty-fifth Anniversary of the Founding of Colored Parkland or "Little Africa"* (1934). Cotter then published two collections of poetry in quick succession, *Collected Poems* (1938) and his *Sequel to "The Pied Piper of Hamelin" and Other Poems* (1939). Both are a mix of new works and previously published material. In 1942 Cotter retired after fifty years of work in the Louisville public school system. He published one more work before he died, a collection of aphorisms, stories, poems, and one-act plays entitled *Negroes and Others at Work and Play* (1947). Cotter died on March 14, 1949.

▧ *Critical Extracts*

R. W. THOMPSON   From brickmaker to bookmaker, from distillery hand to dramatist, from teamster to poetaster, is indeed a far cry, but the seemingly impossible chasm between these radical extremes has been bridged by Joseph Seamon Cotter, the very capable principal of the Eighth street school, Louisville, Ky., and author of *Caleb, the Degenerate*, a dramatic poem; *Links of Friendship*, and many other meritorious productions in verse and prose. He has written some short stories that have been well received. Assuredly, he is a Negro who has "done things" for the moral and intellectual advancement of the race. ⟨. . .⟩

Mr. Cotter is a "born poet" and a happy story-teller. Every sentiment, incident or chain of events illustrative of human nature, appeals to his sensitive mind, and is gathered up by his constructive genius into a finite tale or verse. In English literature and composition he is wholly self-taught. He fell naturally into rhyming when he began to write, but received no instruction beyond the most elementary hints as to meter. Whatever he has done since has been the result of unaided effort. The first paper to give Mr. Cotter's muse a hearing was the *Louisville Courier-Journal*, and it has gladly published many of his contributions from time to time, pronouncing him the peer of Dunbar in the artistic portrayal of Negro character at close range.

Mr. Cotter's *Links of Friendship* (1898) attracted much favorable comment, but a more ambitious work was the dramatic poem *Caleb, the Degenerate* (1900), the literary quality of which has been attested in autograph letters from Israel Zangwill, Maxine Elliott, Mrs. Langtry, De Wolf Hopper, Alfred Austin, England's poet laureate; Charles Chilton, editor of *Chilton's Guide and Racing Mail*, Manchester, England; Harrison Grey Fisk, editor *New York Dramatic Mirror*; James Whitcomb Riley, Booker T. Washington and many others. His occasional verses have been accepted by representative journals which had not previously recognized Negro writers, notably *Suburban Life of Boston*. A new volume, embracing a collection of his later effusions, may be expected soon, in response to popular demand. Mr. Cotter is modest and unassuming in manner, but in the vast borderland of the South, by voice, pen and practical labor, he is accomplishing solid and substantial results that will go far toward giving the Negro an honored place in both the spiritual and the industrial life of the century.

R. W. Thompson, "Negroes Who Are 'Doing Things': Joseph Seamon Cotter," *Alexander's Magazine* 1, No. 4 (15 August 1905): 25–26

JOHN WILSON TOWNSEND   Let no catholic-minded Kentuckian point the finger of scorn at me because I see fit to make an appreciative note on Joseph S. Cotter, the Louisville Negro poet. If one will read ⟨Cotter⟩, one will agree with the present writer that, although the poet's color be black, he deserves a deal of recognition from those who care for clever verse, if not poetry of the highest order.

The Kentucky Negro, it is interesting at this time to note, has his representatives in the major departments of literature. In history and biography he is represented by John H. Jackson and William J. Simmons; in fiction by W. W. Brown and A. A. Whitman; and in poetry, both lyric and dramatic, by George M. McClellan, Henry A. Laine, and Joseph S. Cotter. ⟨. . .⟩

Cotter has published three books. His first, entitled *Links of Friendship*, appeared in 1898; his second, called *Caleb, the Degenerate*, is a four-act drama; and his latest book, issued in 1909, *A White Song and a Black One*. A rather creditable showing for a Kentucky Negro, is it not? ⟨. . .⟩

Charles J. O'Malley, the Kentucky poet and critic, stated the difference between Dunbar and Cotter: "Dunbar, perhaps, displays more of the poet's stock-in-trade, blue skies, bird-songs, brooks, roses, green grass; Cotter, we

incline to think, soberer thought, deeper philosophy, and certainly a clearer
spiritual insight."

John Wilson Townsend, "Kentucky's Dunbar," *Lore of the Meadowland* (Lexington,
KY: Press of J. L. Richardson & Co., 1911), pp. 23–24, 26–27

ROBERT T. KERLIN   It was at Bardstown, February 2, 1861, that
Joseph Seamon Cotter was born. Let Bardstown be put on the literary map
of America, not because Stephen Collins Foster wrote "My Old Kentucky
Home" there, but because one was born there the latchet of whose poetic
shoes he was not worthy to unloose. "A poet, a bard, to be born in Bardstown—how odd, and how appropriate!" one exclaims. And *bard* seems
exactly the right appellation for this song-maker and story-man. But it is
not altogether so. In character bardlike, but not in appearance. Bards have
long, unkempt, white hair, which mingles with beards that rest on their
bosoms. Cotter's square-cut chin is clean-shaven, and his large brain-dome
shows like a harvest moon. But he makes poems and invents and discovers
stories, and, bard-like, recites or relates them to whatever audience may
call for them—in schools, in churches, at firesides. Minus the hairy habili-
ments he is a bard. ⟨. . .⟩

Like Dunbar, Cotter is a satirist of his people—or certain types of his
people—a gentle, humorous, affectionate satirist. His medium for satire is
dialect, inevitably. Sententious wisdom, irradiated with humor, appears in
these pieces in homely garb. In standard English, without satire or humor
that wisdom thus appears:

> What deeds have sprung from plow and pick!
>   What bank-rolls from tomatoes!
> No dainty crop of rhetoric
>   Can match one of potatoes.

The gospel of work has been set forth by our poet in a four-act poetic
drama entitled *Caleb, the Degenerate*. All the characters are Negroes. The
form is blank verse—blank verse of a very high order, too. The language, like
Shakespeare's—though Browning rather than Shakespeare is suggested—is
always that of a poet. The wisdom is that of a man who has observed closely
and pondered deeply. Idealistic, philosophical, poetical—such it is. It bears
witness to no ordinary dramatic ability.

"Best bard, because the wisest," says our Israfel. Verily. "Sage" you may
call this man as well as "bard." The proof is in poems and tales, apologues

and apothegms. 〈. . .〉 His nature is opulent—the cultivation began late and the harvest grows richer.

> Robert T. Kerlin, *Negro Poets and Their Poems* (Washington, DC: Associated Publishers, 1923), pp. 73, 79–80

GERALD BRADLEY   Probably the first play of the period to deal solely with a Negro theme was *Caleb, the Degenerate,* written by a Negro, Joseph S. Cotter, Sr., and published in 1903 in Louisville. A moral lesson on the dangers of depravity, its purpose was to influence officials of Tuskegee Institute to concentrate on practical training, rather than book learning. Although written in a terribly inept blank verse, it is perhaps the closest thing to a folk play ever turned out in the United States; by which I mean, it is obviously written by a member of the "folk" with the purpose of influencing the "folk" to act in a certain manner. That its "folk" element is hidden behind a blank-verse form is less of a handicap to it than is, say, Paul Green's removal from the "folk"—educationally, economically and physically—during the time he was writing the main body of his "folk" plays.

Like William Wells Brown's plays, however, *Caleb* was never staged; it was read at meetings. In its incidents and dialogue it is frequently laughable, and perhaps it is well that it was left unproduced. Near the end of the play, for example, Olivia, a poor but industrious colored girl, is sent to Boston to get money for her foster father's industrial arts school. She returns with $100,000, explaining that "Chance threw me with a group of millionaires" who believed in her cause. Cotter stressed industrial arts, avoidance of politics, the benefits of hard work, and the idea that the Negro was now American, not African.

> Gerald Bradley, "Goodby, Mister Bones: The Emergence of Negro Themes and Characters in American Drama," *Anthology of the American Negro in the Theatre,* ed. Lindsay Patterson (New York: Publishers Company, 1967), p. 15

DORIS E. ABRAMSON   Joseph S. Cotter's play, *Caleb, the Degenerate,* with the amazing subtitle *A Study of the Types, Customs, and Needs of the American Negro,* is one Negro's way of expressing appreciation of Booker T. Washington's point of view. It is a slight, pretentious play, written in blank verse. 〈. . .〉

Joseph Cotter states the purpose of his play in the Author's Preface:

> The aim is to give a dramatic picture of the Negro as he is today.
> The brain and soul of the Negro are rising rapidly. On the other
> hand, there is more depravity among a certain class of Negro than
> ever before. This is not due to anything innate. It is the result of
> unwise, depraved leadership and conditions growing out of it. . . .
> The Negro needs very little politics, much industrial training, and
> a dogged settleness [sic] as far as going to Africa is concerned. To
> this should be added clean, intelligent fireside leadership.

There is no doubt that Cotter listened attentively to Booker T. Washington's "Atlanta Compromise."

Caleb, the Degenerate, which is in four acts, is filled with unbelievable characters spouting incredible lines. There is no moment when they touch reality, even to the extent of characters in ⟨William Wells Brown's⟩ *The Escape* or in early melodramas by white authors writing about Negro characters. There is no minstrel type here, no Cato or Topsy. The characters, forced to speak in blank verse that tries to soar no matter how the vocabulary would pull it down, are merely vessels for ideas. ⟨. . .⟩

None of the characters in the play seem to exist as men but rather to represent types. Caleb and his leader, Rahab, represent wicked types, the degenerate Negroes. Goodness is personified by Olivia and her father, the Bishop. Olivia, in the course of the play, establishes an industrial school for the children of Negroes her father has described as "a people, friendless, ignorant, / living from hand to mouth, from jail to grave." Olivia and the Bishop rise to such an emotional pitch in their enthusiasm for industrial training that they give it credit for "health, wealth, morals, literature, civilization." Somehow one senses that even Booker T. Washington would not have made such extravagant claims.

Two minority views expressed by depraved characters are that Negroes should vote and that they might consider going back to Africa. The playwright did not consider either viewpoint worth much attention. The Bishop refers to his people as "primitive people" and seems to conclude that suffrage is beyond them at the moment. He recognizes, however, that they are Americans—"And this land shall be our paradise"—not Africans.

The degenerate Caleb is found dead of his profligacy in the woods on the grounds of Olivia's industrial school. His death is represented as being horrible because he followed the wicked Rahab who professed to lead, not to love, his race. Had Caleb listened to Olivia and the Bishop, he might have reaped the benefits of the school, which Olivia says was built with gifts from millionaires. He might at least have been able to go to war with Dude, who at the very end of the play announces:

> I go to war. Some say the Negro shirks
> The tasks of peace. Who says he will not fight?
> I go to war.

Joseph Cotter set out to write a moral tract that would show the dangers of depravity and the values of industrial training over mere book learning—"Go, cage life's life before you pause to read." He put into the play good and bad characters, drew his message, killed off the wicked, rewarded the virtuous, and even, in conclusion, waved the American flag.

Doris E. Abramson, *Negro Playwrights in the American Theatre 1925–1959* (New York: Columbia University Press, 1969), pp. 15–17

JAMES V. HATCH   Yes, Mr. Cotter is urging the black man to follow Dr. Washington's work ethic ⟨in *Caleb, the Degenerate*⟩. As has been suggested, the race virulence of America was at a crest in Cotter's time. Solutions for survival had to be found. Yes, the play was written with an eye to the white reader. The preface to the play was composed by Thomas Watkins, financial editor of the Louisville *Courier-Journal*, who wrote, "The author is one of a face that has given scarcely anything of literature to the world." How pleased Mr. Watkins must have been to help a good nigra. But although the surface features of the play were meant for the white and black readers who already believed, there is a subsurface that commands the attention of those aware of the black experience.

The failure of the critics to find much merit in *Caleb* is a failure to recognize this subsurface of black experience, a powerful intensity created out of Joseph Cotter's own growing up in America. Nowhere is this intensity greater than in the character of Caleb.

For the reader who is attracted by the emotional drive of Caleb, it is intriguing to note the author's belated attempt in the fourth act to explain Caleb's degeneracy by shifting the blame to another man.

> DOCTOR: . . . His mother sinned ere he was born
> This tainted him, therefore his wicked course.
> BISHOP: No! No! She did not sin. Caleb was led
> To that belief.
> DOCTOR: Was led?
> BISHOP: Rahab's the man!

The blame is Rahab's, but the motivation for the crime has only been pushed back, not explained. The nature of the "mother's sin" is not clear. Ten years later, Mr. Cotter made it more explicit when he published a collection of short stories. The lead story is entitled "Caleb," and follows the plot of the play in many respects—except that the mother and father of Caleb were married twice: once before and once after emancipation (the slave marriage presumably was not sanctified by church and state). Caleb was born between the marriages, ergo a bastard. When Caleb learns this in the story, he strikes his father "violently over the heart." The father falls dead. ⟨. . .⟩

⟨. . .⟩ Joseph Cotter himself was the bastard son of a black mother and her "employer," a Scotch-Irishman, "a prominent citizen of Louisville." The fact that young Joseph was not sent to school but put to menial work at the age of ten suggests that the "prominent citizen" did not rejoice in his Negro son. It is fair to speculate that Cotter's black experience as the bastard black son of a white father speaks through both Rodney ⟨in "Rodney"⟩ and Caleb.

⟨. . .⟩ Joseph Cotter hated his Anglo-Saxon father, and by extension, the country he attempts to praise in act three. A comparison of the Old Man's speeches, as he urges his followers to leave "a country that is one ignoble grave," with those of the Bishop, who is defending America as a paradise, makes the latter appear vacuous. ⟨. . .⟩

How much Mr. Cotter is aware of his own dual attitude regarding white America must be left to the reader—with one final hint. What is the real allegory of the scene in act two between the Bishop, Olivia, and the ministers? Is this a "realistic" scene, or did Mr. Cotter write a surrealistic scene of associative visual and aural images? If the scene were transferred to *Alice in Wonderland* (and it could easily be done), would it not become "significant?"

Perhaps the case that the author was consciously disguising his material can never be proved. Indeed, it may not be possible to show that some of the best scenes of the play sprang "unintended" from his unconscious. However, a fair and sensitive reading will reveal that Joseph Cotter is a black man whose total being is writing out the anguish of his life. It may be enough that he saw early that for the black man to have power he must own the means of distribution and production. And perhaps the fairytale ending was Mr. Cotter's final note of satire on what might be expected from the great white fathers.

James V. Hatch, "*Caleb the Degenerate*," *Black Theater, U.S.A.: 45 Plays by Black Americans 1847–1974*, ed. James V. Hatch (New York: Free Press, 1974), pp. 62–63

JOAN R. SHERMAN   During five decades of poetry-writing, Cotter's interests range from industrial education in the 1890's to the "zoot suit" and atom bomb in 1947. In both dialect and standard English verse he urges social and moral reform, sectional reconciliation, and brotherhood. He satirizes the foibles and frailties of blacks but also praises their strengths and accomplishments; he philosophically examines God's ways and mysteries of human nature; he comments on historical events and pays homage to notables like Frederick Douglass, William Lloyd Garrison, Cassius M. Clay, Presidents McKinley, Taft, and Roosevelt, Booker T. Washington, and W. E. B. Du Bois; he extols good literature and his literary idols: Shakespeare, Milton, Tennyson, Riley, Holmes, Winburne, Poe, and his close friend Dunbar. Finally, Cotter writes story ballads and light verse enlivened by wit and striking imagery.

Cotter's major concern is race advancement, to be gained by a mixture of race pride, humility, hard work, education, and a positive, optimistic outlook. He chides lazy, aggressive, extravagant, and parasitical blacks who will never succeed in "The Loafing Negro," "The Don't-Care Negro," "The Vicious Negro," "I'se Jes' er Little Nigger," and "Negro Love Song." He praises those who are moving upward in "Ned's Psalm of Life for the Negro"; in "The Negro Woman," which charges the female "To give the plan, to set the pace, / Then lead him in the onward race"; and in "The True Negro":

> Though black or brown or white his skin,
> He boldly holds it is no sin,
> So long as he is true within,
>   To be a Negro.
>
> . . . .
>
> He loves his place, however humbling,
> He moves by walking, not by stumbling,
> He lives by toiling, not by grumbling
>   At being a Negro.

Devoted to the ideology of Washington, Cotter advocates self-help, money-getting, and accommodation in verses like "Tuskegee," "The Negro's Educational Creed," and "Dr. Booker T. Washington to the National Negro Business League":

> Let's spur the Negro up to work,
>   And lead him up to giving.
> Let's chide him when he fain would shirk,
>   And show him when he's living.
>
> . . . .

What deeds have sprung from plow and pick!
    What bank rolls from tomatoes;
No dainty crop of rhetoric
    Can match one of potatoes.

            .   .   .   .

A little gold won't mar our grace,
    A little ease our glory.
This world's a better biding place
    When money clinks its story.

Caleb, the Degenerate (1903), a four-act play in blank verse subtitled, "A Study of the Types, Customs, and Needs of the American Negro," dramatizes the credo of Cotter's preface: "The Negro needs very little politics, much industrial training, and a dogged settledness as far as going to Africa is concerned. To this should be added clean, intelligent fireside leadership."

Cotter introduces the characters as archetypal Negroes: Caleb, a money-hungry atheist, murders his father, philosophizes in pun-ridden Elizabethan diction, goes mad, and dies; Rahab, an amoral politician and emigrationist, corrupts everyone. Caleb and Rahab typify "unwise, depraved leadership." In contrast, the "highest types" are a magniloquent Bishop and his daughter Olivia, who teaches in the industrial school and unwisely loves Caleb. The Bishop sprinkles abstruse theological arguments with homilies: "Industrial training is the thing at last," "God's love and handicraft must save the world," "Work is the basis of life's heritage." Olivia, who has written a book, *The Negro and His Hands*, idealizes "hewers of wood and drawers of water" and the true religion:

Hope is the star that lights self unto self.
Faith is the hand that clutches self's decree.
Mercy is oil self keeps for its own ills.
Justice is hell made present by a blow.

Although *Caleb* is poor drama and mediocre poetry, it is probably the most original tract supporting Washington's policies and as such has considerable sociohistorical interest.

Joan R. Sherman, "Joseph Seamon Cotter, Sr.," *Invisible Poets: Afro-Americans of the Nineteenth Century* (Urbana, University of Illinois Press, 1974), pp. 166–68

ANN ALLEN SHOCKLEY   Cotter's first book, *A Rhyming*, was published in 1895, one year after his friend, Paul Laurence Dunbar, visited the South to be a Thanksgiving guest in his Louisville home. Of this historic occasion, the poet's poet son, Joseph S. Cotter, Jr., wrote: "Here for the first time in the south he [Dunbar] read the Negro dialect poems that afterwards made him famous."

The effect of Dunbar's visit apparently had a great influence on the writing style of Cotter, which was indicative in his *A Rhyming* and subsequent works. The poems of Cotter in dialect, such as "The Don't-Care Negro," "Negro Love Song," and "Big Ike and Little Ike," reflect Dunbar phonetically as well as in satire. Cotter's penchant for writing poems about race leaders, "Dr. Booker T. Washington to the National Negro Business League" and "Frederick Douglass," also followed in the vein of Dunbar.

Without a doubt, the Dunbar visit to Louisville and meeting with Cotter was an inspirational one to the burgeoning local poet and made for a lasting friendship. Following the eventful trip, Dunbar became charmed with the south and wrote the poem "After a Visit," which told of his impressionistic stay:

> I BE'N down in ole Kentucky
>   Fur a week er two, an' say,
> 'T wuz ez hard ez breakin' oxen
>   Fur to tear myse'f away.
> Allus argerin' 'bout fren'ship
>   Ah' yer hospitality—
> Y' ain't no right to talk about it
>   Tell you be'n down there to see.

Cotter, who had a writing habit of responding in kind, composed a poem entitled "Answer to Dunbar's 'After a Visit to Kentucky,'" wherein he replied:

> So, you be'n to ole Kentucky,
>   An' you want to go ag'in?
> Well, Kentucky 'll doff her kerchief
>   An' politely ask you in.

As a contemporary of Dunbar, Cotter did not go unnoticed. A poem commemorating the two black poets, one nationally heralded and the other relatively unknown, was penned by a young Kentuckian, James Edgar French. Comparing Dunbar and Cotter as "foster-brothers," French acclaimed them: "The first two Negroes who have dared to climb / Parnassus' mount, and carve your name in rhyme;" ("Dunbar and Cotter").

Cotter's poems were highly influenced similarly by white writers. His "Sequel to the 'Pied Piper of Hamelin'" clearly reflects the metrical rhythmic rhyming of Browning. Cotter's admiration of Tennyson, Emerson, Bacon, and James W. Riley was made known in his poems with titles bearing their names: "Alfred Tennyson," "Emerson," "Bacon," and "On Hearing James W. Riley Read." To Riley, he acknowledged: "To tell the truth, each piece he read / Set up a jingle in my head."

Ann Allen Shockley, "Joseph S. Cotter, Sr.: Biographical Sketch of a Black Louisville Bard," CLA Journal 18, No. 3 (March 1975): 327–29

EUGENE B. REDMOND   In his life and work, Cotter looks forward to Blacks like Du Bois, James Weldon Johnson, Mary McLeod Bethune, and Langston Hughes. In his writings, he anticipates the variety and virtuosity of a Dunbar. For, in the words of one critic of the period, "he makes poems and invents and discovers stories, and bardlike, recites them to whatever audience may call for them—in schools, in churches, at firesides" (Kerlin). Brilliant, precocious and enduring, Cotter pursued the complex side of life, daring to examine the often oversimplified phenomenon of race relations in America. Kerlin said of his work: "Some are tragedies and some are comedies and some are tragi-comedies of everyday life among the Negroes."

Cotter (Brown says he has "both point and pith"), it must be said, was among the first black poets to represent, without shame and minstrelsy, authentic black folk life. He wrote in formal—academic, bookish—structures; but he also wrote explicitly in dialect and standard English, of common life and common problems. He achieves "rushing rhythms and ingenious rhymes" when he is at his best; and a quiet, reflective perseverance when he writes introspectively. A disciple of Dunbar, Cotter is able to capture vividly the theme of traveling and weariness that pervades so much black literature and song (see "The Way-Side Well" and repetitions that establish the drudgery and the momentum to carry on). He can be satirical and admonishing in dialect, as in "The Don't-Care Negro":

> Neber min' your manhood's risin'
>   So you habe a way to stay it.
> Neber min' folks' good opinion
>   So you have a way to slay it.

In "The Negro Child" Cotter tells the youth to let "lessons of stern yester-days"

> . . . be your food, your drink, your rest,

and in the same poem he strikes a pose similar to that of Booker T. Washington's when he advises the child to

> Go train your head and hands to do,
> Your head and heart to dare.

Cotter's verses also exalt black and liberal white heroes ("Frederick Douglass," "Emerson," "The Race Welcomes Dr. W. E. B. Du Bois as Its Leader," "Oliver Wendell Holmes") and relish such experiences as reading or listening to Dunbar ("Answer to Dunbar's 'After a Visit' " and "Answer to Dunbar's 'A Choice' ") and Riley ("On Hearing James Whitcomb Riley Read"). He vigorously searches the human heart—and the intangibles of lying, hating, and self denying—in such poems as "Contradiction" and "The Poet." "My Poverty and Wealth" recalls Corrothers' "Compensation," since the richness and strength of commonness, charity and honesty triumph over money and a high social station. ⟨. . .⟩ A good biographical-critical study of Cotter is long overdue.

> Eugene B. Redmond, *Drumvoices: The Mission of Afro-American Poetry* (Garden City, NY: Anchor Press/Doubleday, 1976), pp. 105–6

DICKSON D. BRUCE, JR.   ⟨Cotter's⟩ *Negro Tales* is ⟨. . .⟩ an unusual book. It is a collection of brief stories, some of which are clearly modeled on folktales. Others have less clear roots and show a remarkable departure from traditional literary modes.

Among the stories clearly based on folktales are an African story, "The Jackal and the Lion," and an Afro-American animal tale with the descriptive title "How Mr. Rabbit Secures a Pretty Wife and Rich Father-in-Law." Both stories have as their central characters the trickster figure so prominent in African and Afro-American traditions. Another tale, "Kotchin' de Nines," a story about playing the numbers, is introduced by Cotter as "a Negro tale current in Louisville." "Faith in the White Folks" fits in with the large body of black folktales that joke about stereotypes and about the subordinate place of blacks in American society.

Among the writings whose sources are less clear, the one that is closest to other black writing is "Tesney, the Deceived," which self-consciously reflects on traditional literary treatments of racial mixture. ⟨. . .⟩

"Tesney" is a strange story, filled with a grotesqueness utterly unknown in black writing before or during Cotter's time. ⟨. . .⟩ It may simply be that Cotter was an eccentric, at least when he put pen to paper, although there is no corroborating evidence. It may also be that Cotter was, to some extent, drawing on oral sources for "Tesney." Stylistically, the tale shares much with common practices in oral story-telling. Folklorists such as Linda Degh and Daniel Crowley have made much of the ways in which traditional storytellers improvise, deal in the fantastic, and shift scenes radically and abruptly—all in an effort to keep their audiences entertained.

One may see all of this in Cotter's story. Elements of the fantastic appear in, for example, the kind of exaggeration that makes Agnes a 350-pound woman and the grotesquerie of Tesney's burying her baby alive and later digging it up. The flow of the narrative has an improvised quality that likewise resembles oral tradition. One sees this clearly in an account of Tesney's torment after she has buried the baby. ⟨. . .⟩ The coming of the storm and the "Voice of the Clouds" enter the story only at this point, an abrupt scene setting much like the abrupt shift when the story moves from Tesney's search for her white father to her problems with Agnes and George.

The same may be said of what is certainly the strangest story in Cotter's collection, a tale entitled "Rodney." This is the story of an illegitimate child whose mother is black and whose father is white. Rodney meets his father only once ⟨. . .⟩

Following this meeting, most of the story takes place on a single day in Rodney's home. ⟨. . .⟩ The family is ⟨. . .⟩ visited by a "professor," who is trying to get Rodney to go to school. He, too, treats Rodney and Rodney's mother with contempt. Rodney offers the professor a drink, then tells him that the women have spit into the glass. His little sister, Mary, goes further, telling the professor that the women "puked into it." After a debate over the difference between spitting and puking, the professor runs from the house, and the family recognizes the love each member has for the others. A satire on black snobbery, this story, too relies on the sort of grotesquerie, exaggeration, and improvisation that marks much of oral tradition.

Thus it is quite possible that even "Tesney" and "Rodney" had some background in oral tradition, although one cannot trace them to conventional sources in Afro-American folklore. Cotter was fond of telling stories and even organized story-telling sessions and story-telling contests for black children in Louisville. But, in any case, his collection *Negro Tales* offered a striking departure from older modes, even in the language Cotter chose to write down, and showed a willingness to portray a version of black life that was rather far from the images created by earlier writers, even those in the dialect tradition.

Dickson D. Bruce, Jr., *Black American Writing from the Nadir: The Evolution of a Literary Tradition 1877–1915* (Baton Rouge: Louisiana State University Press, 1989), pp. 195–98

◈ *Bibliography*

A Rhyming. 1895.

Links of Friendship. 1898.

*Caleb, the Degenerate: A Play in Four Acts: A Study of the Types, Customs,
        and Needs of the American Negro.* 1903.

Sequel to "The Pied Piper of Hamelin." c. 1906.

A White Song and a Black One. 1909.

Negro Tales. 1912.

*Twenty-fifth Anniversary of the Founding of Colored Parkland or "Little Africa,"
        Louisville, Ky.* 1934.

Collected Poems. 1938.

Sequel to "The Pied Piper of Hamelin" and Other Poems. 1939.

Negroes and Others at Work and Play. 1947.

Paul Laurence Dunbar
1872–1906

PAUL LAURENCE DUNBAR was born in Dayton, Ohio, on June 27, 1872, the son of former slaves. He attended a local high school where he was the only black enrolled and was the editor of the school paper. After school Dunbar worked as an elevator boy in Dayton but also began to contribute poems and stories to local newspapers. He met Charles Thatcher, a lawyer from Toledo who gave substantial support in launching his literary career. Dunbar also worked as a clerk in the Haitian Pavilion at the World's Columbian Exposition in Chicago, where he met Frederick Douglass and other prominent black figures.

Dunbar published poems in Dayton newspapers and brought out two verse collections, *Oak and Ivy* and *Majors and Minors*, privately printed in 1893 and 1895, respectively. William Dean Howells's influential review of the latter in *Harper's Weekly* marked the beginning of Dunbar's fame as a poet on a national level. Howells also wrote the introduction to Dunbar's next collection, *Lyrics of Lowly Life* (1896), which was well received. In 1897 Dunbar ventured to England for public readings and met and collaborated with composer Samuel Coleridge-Taylor. Later that year he became employed as reading room assistant in the Library of Congress in Washington, D.C.

In 1898 Dunbar married Alice Ruth Moore, herself a noted poet and short story writer. In that same year he published his first novel, *The Uncalled*, followed by three others in rapid succession: *The Love of Landry* (1900), *The Fanatics* (1901), and *The Sport of the Gods* (1902). In 1899 he participated with Booker T. Washington and W. E. B. Du Bois in readings to raise funds for the Tuskegee Institute, a Southern college for black American students; the following year he took part in Du Bois's conferences on black American issues at Atlanta University. Dunbar also retained a fondness for the Republican party, and in particular Theodore Roosevelt; he participated in this president's inaugural parades, and in 1905 he wrote a poem for the candidate's campaign.

Dunbar's health began to fail around 1900 and he died of tuberculosis on February 8, 1906. His *Complete Poems* was published in 1913. Dunbar was most admired in his own time, and is best remembered today, for his poems and stories written in black dialect. He was the first black author to employ this device, and was inspired, in part, by the example of Robert Burns.

▣ *Critical Extracts*

W. D. HOWELLS   What struck me in reading Mr. Dunbar's poetry was what had already struck his friends in Ohio and Indiana, in Kentucky and Illinois. They had felt, as I felt, that however gifted his race had proven itself in music, in oratory, in several of the other arts, here was the first instance of an American negro who had evinced innate distinction in literature. In my criticism of his book ⟨*Majors and Minors*⟩ I had alleged Dumas in France, and I had forgetfully failed to allege the far greater Pushkin in Russia; but these were both mulattoes, who might have been supposed to derive their qualities from white blood vastly more artistic than ours, and who were the creatures of an environment more favorable to their literary development. So far as I could remember, Paul Dunbar was the only man of pure African blood and of American civilization to feel the negro life aesthetically and express it lyrically. It seemed to me that this had come to its most modern consciousness in him, and that his brilliant and unique achievement was to have studied the American negro objectively, and to have represented him as he found him to be, with humor, with sympathy, and yet with what the reader must instinctively feel to be entire truthfulness. I said that a race which had come to this effect in any member of it, had attained civilization in him, and I permitted myself the imaginative prophecy that the hostilities and the prejudices which had so long constrained his race were destined to vanish in the arts; that these were to be the final proof that God had made of one blood all nations of men. I thought his merits positive and not comparative; and I held that if his black poems had been written by a white man, I should not have found them less admirable. I accepted them as an evidence of the essential unity of the human race, which does not think or feel black in one and white in another, but humanly in all.

Yet it appeared to me then, and it appears to me now, that there is a precious difference of temperament between the races which it would be a great pity ever to lose, and that this is best preserved and most charmingly suggested by Mr. Dunbar in those pieces of his where he studies the moods and traits of his race in its own accent of our English. We call such pieces dialect pieces for want of some closer phrase, but they are really not dialect so much as delightful personal attempts and failures for the written and spoken language. In nothing is his essentially refined and delicate art so well shown as in these pieces, which, as I ventured to say, described the range between appetite and emotion, with certain lifts far beyond and above it, which is the range of the race. He reveals in these a finely ironical perception of the negro's limitations, with a tenderness for them which I think so very rare as to be almost quite new. I should say, perhaps, that it was this humorous quality which Mr. Dunbar had added to our literature, and it would be this which would most distinguish him, now and hereafter.

W. D. Howells, "Introduction" (1896), *The Complete Poems of Paul Lawrence Dunbar* (New York: Dodd, Mead, 1913), pp. viii–x

---

ROBERT T. KERLIN   Dunbar is a fact, as Burns, as Whittier, as Riley, are facts—a fact of great moment to a people and for a people. ⟨. . .⟩ I mention Dunbar here only to draw attention to my theme, that theme being, not one poet, but a multitude animated by one spirit though characterized by diversity of talent, all spokesmen of their race in its new era. Dunbar does indeed appear to sustain a definite relation to these black singers of the new day. For one thing, he revealed to the Negro youth of our land the latent literary powers of their race, and, not less important, he revealed also the poetic materials at hand in the Negro people, lowly or distinguished. He may therefore be thought of as the fecundating genius of their muses. But I think they are born, as he was, of the creative zeitgeist, sent of heaven.

But to give my assertion regarding Dunbar its proper significance, I must remark, for white people, that there were two Dunbars, and that they know but one. There is the Dunbar of "the jingle in a broken tongue," whom Howells with gracious but imperfect sympathy and understanding brought to the knowledge of the world, and whom the public readers, white and black alike (the sin is upon both), have found it delightful to present, to the entire eclipse of the other Dunbar. That other Dunbar was the poet of the flaming "Ode to Ethiopia," the pathetic lyric, "We Wear the Mask," and a score of other pieces in which, using their speech, he matches himself with the poets who shine as stars in the firmament of our admiration. This Dunbar, I say, Howells failed to appreciate, and ignorance of him has been fostered by professional readers and writers. The first Dunbar, the generally accepted one, was, as Howells pointed out, the artistic interpreter of the old fashioned, vanishing generation of black folk—the generation that was maimed and scarred by slavery, that presented so many ludicrous and pathetic, abject and lovable aspects in strange mixture. The second Dunbar was the prophet robed in a mantle of austerity, shod with fire, bowed with sorrow, as every true prophet has been, in whatever time, among whatever people. He was the prophet, I say, of a new generation, a coming generation, as he was the poet of a vanishing generation. The generation of which he was the prophet-herald has arrived. Its most authentic representatives are the poets to whom I have referred.

> Robert T. Kerlin, *Contemporary Poetry of the Negro* (Hampton, VA: Hampton Norman & Agricultural Institute, 1921), pp. 6–7

BENJAMIN BRAWLEY   Dunbar's conception of his art was based on his theory of life. He felt that he was first of all a man, then an American, and incidentally a Negro. To a world that looked upon him primarily as a Negro and wanted to hear from him simply in his capacity as a Negro, he was thus a little difficult to understand. He never regarded the dialect poems as his best work, and, as he said in the eight lines entitled "The Poet," when one tried to sing of the greatest themes in life, it was hard to have the world praise only "a jingle in a broken tongue." His position was debatable, of course, but that was the way he felt. At the meeting at the Waldorf-Astoria a reporter asked about the quality of the poetry written by Negroes as compared with that of white people. Dunbar replied, "The predominating power of the African race is lyric. In that I should expect the writers of my race to excel. But, broadly speaking, their poetry will not be exotic or differ much from that of the whites. . . . For two hundred and fifty years the environment of the Negro has been American, in every respect the same as that of all other Americans." "But isn't there," continued the interviewer, "a certain tropic warmth, a cast of temperament that belongs of right to the African race?" "Ah," said the poet, "what you speak of is going to be a loss. It is inevitable. We must write like the white men. I do not mean imitate them; but our life is now the same." Then he added: "I hope you are not one of those who would hold the Negro down to a certain kind of poetry—dialect and concerning only scenes on plantations in the South?"

To a later school of Negro writers, one more definitely conscious of race, Dunbar thus appears as somewhat artificial. The difference is that wrought by the World War. About the close of that conflict Marcus Garvey, by a positively radical program, made black a fashionable color. It was something not to be apologized for, but exploited. Thenceforth one heard much about "the new Negro," and for a while Harlem was a literary capital. In Dunbar's time, however, black was not fashionable. The burden still rested upon the Negro to prove that he could do what any other man could do, and in America that meant to use the white man's technique and meet the white man's standard of excellence. It was to this task that Dunbar addressed himself. This was the test that he felt he had to satisfy, and not many will doubt that he met it admirably.

> Benjamin Brawley, *Paul Laurence Dunbar: Poet of His People* (Chapel Hill: University
> of North Carolina Press, 1936), pp. 76–77

STERLING A. BROWN   As has been pointed out, Dunbar was not the first Negro poet to use dialect, although his predecessors had not realized the possibilities of the medium. The influential work of white authors in Negro dialect, from Stephen Foster and the minstrel song writers through local colorists such as Erwin Russell, J. A. Macon, Joel Chandler Harris and Thomas Nelson Page, will be our concern in the concluding chapters devoted to poetry. In spite of these forerunners, however, Dunbar was not only the first American Negro to "feel the Negro life aesthetically and express it lyrically," as William Dean Howells wrote, but also the first American poet to handle Negro folklife with any degree of fullness. As a portrayal of Negro life, Dunbar's picture has undoubted limitations, but they are by no means so grave as those of Russell and Page. ⟨. . .⟩

Dunbar's best qualities are clear. Such early poems as "Accountability" and "An Antebellum Sermon" show flashes of the unforced gay humor that was to be with him even to the last. With a few well-turned folk phrases he calls up a scene as in "Song of Summer," or

> Tu'key gobbler gwine 'roun' blowin'
> Gwine 'roun' gibbin' sass an' slack
> Keep on talkin' Mistah Tu'key
> You ain't seed no almanac. ("Signs of the Times")

> Tek a cool night, good an' cleah
> Skiff o' snow upon de groun' ("Hunting Song")

Except when unexplainably urged to write Irish dialect or imitate Riley's "Orphant Annie," or to cross misspelling with moralizing as in "Keep A Pluggin' Away," his grasp upon folk-speech is generally sure. His rhythms almost never stumble and are frequently catchy: at times as in "Itching Heels" he gets the syncopation of a folk dance. Most of all he took up the Negro peasant as a clown, and made him a likeable person.

> Sterling A. Brown, *Negro Poetry and Drama* (Washington, DC: Associates in Negro Folk Education, 1937), pp. 32, 35

VICTOR LAWSON Dunbar could achieve, in his verse in literary English, a sophisticated humour, sometimes mock-heroic, sometimes tragi-comic, sometimes facetious and sometimes grim. He could write society verse too poignant to be maudlin, despite the double handicap of American Victorianism and second-generation respectability. He recounted his own intense experiences of love and life in a few poems in which the clichés disappeared or "became again sincere." He wrote a superlative lyric to one who was the "soul of a summer's day" in which the ideas of evanescence and a suggestion of mutability were touchingly expressed. He profoundly analyzed the intellectual processes in "Why Fades a Dream," to which he added the Gothic reveries of one about to fall asleep, in "Ere Sleep Comes Down." The best of his poetry on nature was marked by fancy based on originality of the point of view, carried out probably as well as its potentialities allow. The best among the fables, "Dawn," merits 16th century praise as being based on one of the purest and best conceits of our language. Finally, the religious poetry has in "Weltschmerz" an example of haunting metaphor, "intriguing" paradox and enigma and ethical suggestiveness as an overtone of a universal appealing tableau.

> Victor Lawson, *Dunbar Critically Examined* (Washington, DC: Associated Publishers, 1941), pp. 48–49

ARNA BONTEMPS Paul Lawrence Dunbar, a son of former slaves, appeared about 120 years after Phillis Wheatley and greeted the twentieth century with several volumes of lyrics, including such representative poems as "Dawn," "The Party," "We Wear the Mask," and "Compensation," together with scores of others which, more than a half-century later, have a host of admirers to whom they remain fresh and poignant. His *Complete Poems*, 1913, is still in print.

A strong sense of melody and rhythm was a feature of Dunbar's poetry, as it has been of nearly all the Negro poets of the United States. Dunbar's delightful country folk, his broad, often humorous, dialect failed to create a tradition, however. Later Negro poets have held that the effective use of dialect in poetry is limited to humor and pathos. Accordingly, most of them have abandoned it.

> Arna Bontemps, "Introduction," *American Negro Poetry* (New York: Hill & Wang, 1963), p. xv

---

DARWIN TURNER   Even if Dunbar had been completely free to write scathing protest about the South, he could not have written it, or would have written it ineptly. His experiences and those of his family had not compelled him to hate white people as a group or the South as a region. After Dunbar was twenty, every major job he secured, every publication, and all national recognition resulted directly from the assistance of white benefactors. It is not remarkable that Dunbar assumed that successful Negroes need such help or that, knowing the actuality of Northern benefactors, he believed in the existence of their Southern counterparts. Dunbar was not a unique disciple of such a creed. In *The Ordeal of Mansart*, the militant W. E. B. Du Bois has described the manner in which intelligent freedmen sought salvation with the assistance of Southern aristocrats.

As his personal experiences freed him from bitterness towards Caucasians as a group, so his family's experiences relieved bitterness towards the South. The experiences of his parents in slavery probably had been milder than most. His father had been trained in a trade and had been taught to read, write, and compute. As a semi-skilled worker occasionally hired out, he fared better than the average field hand. Irony rather than bitterness is the dominant tone in "The Ingrate," a story Dunbar based on his father's life. Although Dunbar's mother had experienced unpleasantness (as what slave did not), her life as a house slave in Kentucky undoubtedly was easier than that of a slave in the deeper South.

Even had his experiences prompted protest against the South, his social and economic philosophies would have militated against it. Believing that America would prosper only if all citizens recognized their interdependence, he sought to win respect for Negroes by showing that, instead of sulking about the past, they were ready to participate in the joint effort to create a new America. In the poems of *Majors and Minors* (1895) and the stories of *Folks from Dixie* (1898), he repeatedly emphasized the ability and willingness of Negroes to forgive white Americans for previous injustices.

Dunbar's noble sentiments and protagonists reveal not only a naive political philosophy but also a romantic and idealized concept of society. He believed in right rule by an aristocracy based on birth and blood which assured culture, good breeding, and all the virtues appropriate to a gentleman. He further believed that Negroes, instead of condemning such a society, must prove themselves worthy of a place in it by showing that they had civilized themselves to a level above the savagery which he assumed to be characteristic of Africa. Furthermore, having been reared in Dayton, Ohio, he distrusted big cities and industrialization. Provincially, he assumed the good life for the uneducated to be the life of a farmer in a small western or mid-western settlement or the life of a sharecropper for a benevolent Southern aristocrat. Neither a scholar, political scientist, nor economist, he naively offered an agrarian myth as a shield against the painful reality of discrimination in cities. ⟨. . .⟩

In summary, Dunbar's experiences, his social and economic philosophies, and his artistic ideals limited his criticism of the South. This fact, however, should not imply, as some suppose, that Dunbar accepted the total myth of the plantation tradition. In reality, he was no more willing to assume the romanticized plantation to be characteristic of the entire South than he was willing to deny that some slaves had loved their masters or had behaved foolishly.

> Darwin Turner, "Paul Laurence Dunbar: The Rejected Symbol," *Journal of Negro History* 52, No. 1 (January 1967): 2–4

ADDISON GAYLE, JR.   Despite the importance of *A Career* to Dunbar's development as a poet, few of his biographers have realized its full implication. Had they done so, they might have noted that Dunbar's most serious poems in *Oak and Ivy* were written in standard English and that the poet himself was less than pleased with the success of his dialect pieces. ⟨. . .⟩

Dunbar never took these poems seriously. For him they were humorous ditties written to entertain white audiences. Few black people could afford to spend a dollar for his book. Therefore, he was able to sell enough copies to repay his debt three weeks after publication only because of the book's popularity with whites. They bought copies for themselves and sent others

to their friends. Some, like Attorney Thatcher and Dr. Tobey, were sophisticated men who differentiated between the humorous poems and the more
serious ones. As for the others, he tried to instruct them. His title was his
way of choosing between his poems in dialect and those in standard English.
He thought of a tree with ivy growing all about it. The tree was more
important than the ivy, for the ivy was neither strong nor functional, but
merely useless ornamentation. So, too, was the ivy of his book—the dialect
poems—ornamentation to the sturdy oak—the poems in standard English.
Only later in life was he to learn that within this title he had planted the
seeds of a truer metaphor; that of the ivy engulfing the oak, strangling the
life out of it, so that in time what was at first ornament replaced the
dominant element, and was admired as if it had always been the more
important of the two.

> Addison Gayle, Jr., *Oak and Ivy: A Biography of Paul Laurence Dunbar* (Garden City,
> NY: Doubleday, 1971), pp. 29–31

HOUSTON A. BAKER, JR.   Our critical ambivalence veers in

favor of the poet. At this point, however, we must recall Wilde's dictum
that great art is always in advance of its age, and common sense and our
own literary awareness tell us that great individuals always transcend the
group that provides their maturing and value. In short, the literary master,
the genius, is never of a particular epoch, and with this in mind, one might
acknowledge that Dunbar was neither literary master nor a man of genius.
The counterbalancing factors—a militantly rebellious spirit and a keen
perception of the conditions of artistic greatness along with a Keatsian desire
to achieve it—which might have lifted the poet above his age were absent
in the life of Dunbar. Hence, the first black American poet of distinction
remains an artist rooted in time and incomprehensible without a thorough
understanding of the age that provided the symbols for his art. ⟨. . .⟩

The vitality, humor, communality, protest, acuity, idiom, and fused
strength that characterized the southern, agrarian black folk find expression
in a number of poems that are incredible for their melodiousness and finish.
"Philosophy," "An Ante-Bellum Sermon," "The Party," and "When Malindy Sings" are but four of the poems in which Dunbar captures the best of
both worlds; he is the accomplished American writer, and he is an honest
spokesman for the folk. The results may appear simple, but that is one of
the traits of fine art—a seeming ease of composition. In actuality, the skilled
blending of southern folk regionalism with a conscious literary tradition has

reached high points in the work of some of the most notable American authors—Langston Hughes, Jean Toomer, Sterling Brown, Erskine Caldwell, and William Faulkner. Thus Dunbar points, on occasion, to the classics of the twentieth century, and the merger of the folk and the conscious literary traditions that he brought about has provided one of the most important facets of black American literature from his day to the present.

We are left with a portrait of an artist who gave to humanity a gift of example: a paradigm of the creative spirit overcoming mammoth odds. And at times Dunbar's verse breaks from the confines of a narrow and distorted framework. The better poems serve as correctives to the flaccid romanticism and false antebellum sentimentalism that infused the age in which they were written. They provided a true picture of a strong and enduring people and point directions for some of the finest literary works of this century. Dunbar's gifts were of value, and with just recognition they must prove permanent.

Houston A. Baker, Jr., "Paul Laurence Dunbar, an Evaluation," *Singers of Daybreak: Studies in Black American Literature* (Washington, DC: Howard University Press, 1974), pp. 39–41

LOUIS D. RUBIN, JR.   It is only rarely, in a poem such as "The Haunted Oak," that Dunbar could begin to use the full subtleties of language to express the range of his feelings. In that poem he drew upon the old ballad form, with its traditional folk-language and the convention of simple rural reference. The literary abstractions of the poetry of genteel idealism were muted by the simplicity of the ballad form; yet because he did not have to restrict his vocabulary and sensibility to the dialect of an uneducated primitive, he could come closer to dealing with his experience. It is a poem about a lynching, and though some of its lines are marred by the poet's inability to break away completely from the habit of stating the ideas instead of letting the images embody the story, it contains some of Dunbar's best verse:

> They'd charged him with the old, old crime
> And set him fast in jail;
> Oh, why does the dog howl all night long,
> And why does the night wind wail?
>
> He prayed his prayer and he swore his oath,
> And he raised his hand to the sky;
> But the beat of hoofs smote on his ear,
> And the steady tread drew nigh.

In its understatement, its irony, and its stark imagery, "The Haunted Oak" is an unusual poem for its time. Though it does not have the compression and poised strength of a poem such as Langston Hughes's "Song to a Dark Girl," it foreshadows something of the artistry with which later black poets could unite social protest and craftsmanship at language. Had Dunbar lived longer—he was in his early thirties when he died—there is reason to believe that he would have moved further away from his initial reliance upon the ornate literary diction of genteel idealism toward a more muscular simplicity of language. Certain of his short lyrics, such as "At the Tavern" and "Death," show a virtuosity in languge that his earlier work lacks.

> Louis D. Rubin, Jr., "The Search for a Language, 1746–1923," *Black Poetry in America: Two Essays in Historical Interpretation* by Blyden Jackson and Louis D. Rubin, Jr. (Baton Rouge: Louisiana State University Press, 1974), pp. 18–19

CHIDI IKONNÉ   Paul Laurence Dunbar's complaints about being compelled to write dialect poems are well known. So also is the lament of his autobiographical poem "The Poet" about the world closing its eyes on the good things he has written only "to praise / A jingle in a broken tongue." The frequency with which he employed either literary English or a language that is nonliterary only in appearance, his rejection of the Whitman of *Leaves of Grass* (1855) and adoption of conventional poetic formats even in dialect pieces, his treatment of some of his Negro folk material à la Erwin Russell, James Whitcomb Riley, and Thomas Nelson Page all show his great desire to be numbered among the mainstream American writers of his age. Yet it will be wrong either to interpret his apparent reluctance to be remembered mainly by his dialect poetry as his disapproval of that part of his work or to regard the pieces themselves as a bunch of insincerity. The legitimacy of dialect as a medium of literary representation of folkways is not in question. What Dunbar complains about is being forced to write nothing but dialect: "I am tired, so tired of dialect, . . . I send out graceful little poems, suited for any of the magazines, but they are returned to me by editors who say, 'We would be very glad to have a dialect poem, Mr. Dunbar, but we do not care for the language composition.' "

In a letter dated 13 July 1895 and addressed to his friend Henry A. Tobey he confesses how his earlier ambition to be a lawyer had "died out before the all-absorbing desire to be a worthy singer of the songs of God and nature." He wishes "to be able to interpret my own people through song and story, and to prove to the many that after all we are more human than

African." Most of his "people" at that time were "lowly" folk; dialect provided him with a more effective means (compared with his poetry in literary English) of demonstrating and, by extension, defending their life-style.

Chidi Ikonné, *From Du Bois to Van Vechten: The Early New Negro Literature 1903–1926* (Westport, CT: Greenwood Press, 1981), p. 51

JOANNE M. BRAXTON   Throughout the Harlem Renaissance, Dunbar remained a model for writers as diverse as Countee Cullen and Langston Hughes, both of whom considered Dunbar a great poet. Langston Hughes wrote his first "Dunbarstyle" folk poem when he was still in high school and published it later in his collection *The Dream Keeper*. Likewise, Cullen eulogized Dunbar with the poem "To Paul Laurence Dunbar," pub-lished in his first collection of poetry, *Color* (1925): Indeed, there was much to bind Dunbar's legacy with the spirit of what some would call "these bad New Negroes." To begin with, there was what James A. Emanuel calls Dunbar's "racial fire," his pride in his blackness and his outcry against the oppression of his people, his well-directed if sometimes too understated anger. Then there is Dunbar's appreciation of the significance of his racial and cultural heritage, his loving depiction of the black man and woman farthest down, and his musical rendition of musical black folk language: in short, his daring creation of something completely original, new and unique—an Afrocentric poetic diction that transcended the racist heritage of the plantation tradition and did more than strive to imitate the Anglo-Saxon literary past. The more avant-garde of the Harlem Renaissance artists especially were to identify with and build upon these Dunbar innovations. Likewise, they would struggle with the demands of a predominantly white readership and its insistence on illustrations of black life that were at times more in keeping with its own taste than with the black writer's quest for the artistic freedom and authenticity.

In the final analysis, it is difficult to answer the question of whether Dunbar *unconsciously* acquiesced to racist stereotypes. One could argue that because the dialect tradition Dunbar inherited was so completely and fully invested with negative and demeaning images of blackness, it was not possible for him to be successful, in every instance, in inverting these associations to "signify" on his received linguistic heritage. Perhaps what Dunbar attempted to do, in the words of contemporary black poet Audre Lorde, was "to dismantle the master's house using the master's tools," an extremely difficult if not impossible task. Despite Dunbar's success in writing dialect poetry, he was rightly uncomfortable with the approval he garnered from mainstream white critics, because he knew that they were deaf to his voice of protest and that they misread his work and praised it for the wrong reasons; they did not possess Dunbar's cultural background, his keen ear, or his sympathetic racial sensibility.

> Joanne M. Braxton, "Introduction," *The Collected Poetry of Paul Laurence Dunbar* (Charlottesville: University of Virginia Press, 1993), pp. xxix–xxx

❖ *Bibliography*

Oak and Ivy. 1893.

Majors and Minors. 1895.

Lyrics of Lowly Life. 1896.

African Romances (with Samuel Coleridge-Taylor). 1897.

Folks from Dixie. 1898.

The Uncalled. 1898.

Dream Lovers. 1898.

Lyrics of the Hearthside. 1899.

Poems of Cabin and Field. 1899.

The Strength of Gideon and Other Stories. 1900.

The Love of Landry. 1900.

Uncle Eph's Christmas: A One Act Negro Musical Sketch (with Will Marion Cook). 1900.

The Fanatics. 1901.

Candle-Lightin' Time. 1901.

The Sport of the Gods. 1902.

Lyrics of Love and Laughter. 1902.

In Old Plantation Days. 1903.

When Malindy Sings. 1903.

The Heart of Happy Hollow. 1904.

Li'l' Gal. 1904.

Lyrics of Sunshine and Shadow. 1905.

Howdy, Honey, Howdy. 1905.

A Plantation Portrait. 1905.

Joggin' Erlong. 1906.

Chris'mus Is a'Comin' and Other Poems. 1907.

Life and Works. Ed. Lina Keck Wiggins. 1907.

Complete Poems. 1913.

Speakin' o' Christmas and Other Christmas and Special Poems. 1914.

Best Stories. Ed. Benjamin Brawley. 1938.

Little Brown Baby: Poems for Young People. Ed. Bertha Rodgers. 1940.

The Paul Laurence Dunbar Reader. Ed. Jay Martin and Gossie H. Hudson. 1975.

I Greet the Dawn. Ed. Ashley Bryan. 1978.

Collected Poetry. Ed. Joanne M. Braxton. 1993.

Jupiter Hammon
1711–c. 1800

JUPITER HAMMON is no longer credited as the first black poet in America (a poem by Lucy Terry evidently predates the earliest of his works), but he is still the first black American to write a significant amount of poetry and prose. He was born in slavery on October 3, 1711, and was one of the many slaves residing with the wealthy landowner and slave trader Henry Lloyd at his manor house (then called Queen's Village) in Oyster Bay, Long Island. His father appears to have been a rebellious slave named Opium, and his mother was probably a slave named Rose, who was sold when Jupiter was a young boy.

Hammon was born around the same time as John Lloyd, Jr., a younger son of Henry Lloyd, and may have received private education with him. In 1730 Hammon nearly died of gout, and the extraordinary efforts made to save his life testify to his value to the Lloyds. Three years later Hammon experienced a religious awakening from Bible readings and attendance of Congregational and Anglican services on Long Island and in Connecticut. At some point he began preaching to fellow blacks and lecturing to both black and white audiences. Although he may have written several more works than we now have, his earliest known published work was the poem *An Evening Thought*, a broadside issued on Christmas of 1760. It was once thought to be the earliest black American poem, until the discovery of Lucy Terry's "Bar Fight" (written in 1746 but not published until 1893).

The Lloyds, supporters of the rebel cause, were forced to flee at the outbreak of the Revolutionary War when British troops occupied their manor. They moved to Hartford, Connecticut, where Hammon's literary work flourished. In 1778 he issued a poem dedicated to Phillis Wheatley, the young black slave poet; in 1779 a work entitled *An Essay on the Ten Virgins* was published, but no copies seem to survive; and in 1782 appeared a prose work, a sermon entitled *A Winter Piece*. A poem commemorating the visit of Prince William (later William IV) to the Lloyd manor house was apparently also written in 1782, but it has not come to light. In 1784 he delivered a lecture, *An Address to the Negroes in the State of New-York*, although it was not published until 1787. By this time the Lloyds had returned to their manor in Oyster Bay, where Hammon worked as a gardener, clerk, and informal banker for the Lloyd sons. He does not appear to have married or had children.

Hammon has come under severe criticism for seeming to acquiesce in the institution of slavery and to urge blacks to seek their freedom only in the afterlife; but a proper reading of the religious symbolism of Hammon's prose and poetic work suggests that he used religious imagery to emphasize such points as the spiritual equality of all people, the need for gradual emancipation of slaves, and the notion of the Revolutionary War as God's judgment upon white slaveowners. This last point is made in a poem, "The Kind Master and Dutiful Servant," appended to *An Evening's Improvement* (1783). He frequently equates blacks with the Jews under their captivity in Egypt. Hammon has been criticized for stating in his *Address* that he himself did not wish to be free; but as a seventy-year-old slave he could have done little to support himself and would probably have been reduced to poverty. The will of Henry Lloyd, who died in 1763, had stipulated that "My old negroes are to be provided for," and Hammon was unwilling to forsake this security.

There is no mention of Hammon in public or private records after 1790, and the reissue of his *Address to the Negroes in the State of New-York* in 1806 suggests that he was dead by this time; but his exact date of death, as well as his place of burial, are unknown.

▧ *Critical Extracts*

OSCAR WEGELIN   As a poet Hammon will certainly not rank among the "Immortals." His verse is stilted, and while some of his rhymings are fairly even, we can easily comprehend that they were written by one not well versed in the art of poesy. They have a sameness which is wearying to the reader and there is too much reiteration, in some cases the same or nearly the same words being employed again and again.

His verse is saturated with a religious feeling not always well expressed, as he did not possess the ability to use the right word at the proper time. Hammon was undoubtedly deeply religious, but his religion was somewhat tinged with narrowness and superstition, a not uncommon fault of the time in which he lived and wrote.

Although grammatically almost perfect, it seems certain that an abler and more experienced hand than his own was responsible for this.

Compared with the verses of Phillis Wheatley, his lines are commonplace and few would care to read them more than once. When we consider, however, that this poor slave had probably no other learning than what he had been enabled to secure for himself during his hours of relaxation from labor, it is surprising that the results are not more meagre. Although his rhymings can hardly be dignified by the name of poetry, they are certainly not inferior to many of the rhymings of his day and generation. ⟨. . .⟩

When we consider that he was probably without any education whatso-ever, we marvel that he accomplished as much as he did. Had he had the advantages of learning possessed by Miss Wheatley, it seems possible that as a poet he would have ranked as her equal, if not her superior. His prose writings were also above the mediocre, but from the testimony of one of his printers he was evidently deficient as a speller.

He stands, however, unique in the annals of American Poetry and his works must not be too harshly judged. The disadvantages under which he composed them were probably far greater than we can imagine.

It seems, however, too bad that his verse is entirely of a religious nature. Much would have been added to its interest had he written about some of the events that were transpiring all around him during the War for Independence and the years that followed that struggle.

He seems to have been content to sing the praises of the Master whom he longed to serve and whose reward he some day expected to receive, and with that end in view he labored to instill the blessings of religion into his less fortunate brethren.

For this his memory should be honored and let the broken lines which fell from his pen be cherished, if for no other reason than that they were written by the first American Negro who attempted to give expression to his thoughts in verse.

Oscar Wegelin, Jupiter Hammon: American Negro Poet (New York: C. F. Heartman, 1915), pp. 19–22

VERNON LOGGINS   It is an interesting coincidence that most of Hammon's poetry was published at Hartford at a time when that Connecticut town was the literary capital of America. But if the neoclassical "Hartford

Wits" read his poems, they no doubt looked upon them as chaotic effusions of crude thoughts poured out in a verse not inappropriate to the cheapest balladry. To the twentieth-century mind, which places a high value on the artlessness of folk poetry, Jupiter Hammon's work takes on a new meaning. There is a strength of wild and native religious feeling in what he wrote, a strength which he achieved without conscious effort. From hearing evangelical sermons and from reading the Bible according to his own untrained fancy, he picked up strange notions regarding salvation, penitential cries, redeeming love, tribunal day, the Holy Word, bounteous mercies. His mystic Negro mind played with these notions; and, endowed with the instinct for music which is so strong in his race, he sang out his impressions in such meters as he had become familiar with in the hymns of Charles Wesley and Augustus Montague Toplady, and in such rimes as for the moment pleased his ear. Indeed, his method of composition must have been that of the unknown makers of the spirituals.

> Vernon Loggins, *The Negro Author: His Development in America* (New York: Columbia University Press, 1931), p. 11

J. SAUNDERS REDDING   Hammon's life was motivated by the compulsion of obedience to his earthly and his heavenly master. Perhaps the inevitability of his position tended to wilt his moral fiber. Perhaps the beneficence of his masters lightened the burden of his bondage. Though he was the first Negro slave to publish an adverse opinion on the institution of slavery, his opinion was robbed of its force by the words "though for my own part I do not wish to be free." Perhaps it was the very weakness of the statement that recommended it for publication. At the same time, however, his hedging was not without its wisdom. He says:

"Now I acknowledge that liberty is a great thing, and worth seeking for, if we can get it honestly; and by our good conduct prevail upon our masters to set us free: though for my own part I do not wish to be free, yet I should be glad if others, especially the young negroes, were to be free; for many of us who are grown up slaves, and have always had masters to take care of us, should hardly know how to take care of themselves. . . . That liberty is a great thing we may know from our own feelings, and we may likewise judge so from the conduct of the white people in the late war. How much money has been spent and how many lives have been lost to defend their liberty! I must say that I have hoped that God would open their eyes, when they were so much engaged for liberty, to think of the state of the poor blacks, and to pity us." ⟨An *Address to the Negroes in the State of New-York*⟩

As to literary values, there is not much to choose between Hammon's poetry and prose. Though he was not without the romantic gift of spontaneity, he lacked any knowledge of metrics and sought only to make rhymes. In prose the artlessness of his construction, the rambling sentences, the repetitions reveal, sometimes at the expense of thought, his not unattractive personality. When he is most lucid there is force in the quaintness of his thought evocative of the highly personal flavor of early American letters.

J. Saunders Redding, *To Make a Poet Black* (Chapel Hill: University of North Carolina Press, 1939), pp. 7–8

CHARLES A. VERTANES   Hammon's ideas appeared at the opportune time, and were readily received by those masters who found slaves profitable and wanted to hold on to them. What a gratuitous service Hammon rendered, and how unwittingly, by his open entertainment of such ideas, to the cause of slavery! His words were a salutary check upon the liberating implications of the headstrong political ideas of the Revolution for that cause. They helped to fasten upon the members of his race the slave morality which made the institution of slavery possible. To this end Hammon was encouraged in his literary activity, and his writings were favored with wide distribution. According to Hammon's own testimony, several of his works published during the Revolution while he was at Hartford "were well received, not only by those of my own colour, but by a number of the white people, who thought they might do good among their servants."

It is understandable why many Negroes during the critical years of the Revolutionary War regarded Hammon a traitor to their race which, of course, he was not. He flatly denied the charge that he "had petitioned to the court of Hartford against freedom," affirming that he had neither meddled nor had been concerned in political affairs, and had never said or done anything, either directly or indirectly, to promote or prevent freedom. But the mere fact that his brethren had readily believed in the charge is significant.

To those slaves whose experience with cruel masters had been one long terrifying nightmare, Hammon's failure to offer no other hope for their liberation than a mere appeal to the reason and conscience of these masters was a manifestation of either inexcusable stupidity or gross wickedness, particularly so when the floodgates of freedom were being pushed open by their white brethren and especially when many of them were sympathetic to their cause. If it were right for the whites to wrest their freedom from their unwilling masters across the ocean, why should it not be equally right for them to join forces and broaden the scope of the struggle to include the liberation of the black man as well? It is quite possible that Hammon was being used as a scapegoat by some whites for the failure to include the cause of the black man's liberation in the overall aims of the Revolution, for the report about his petitioning the court of Hartford against freedom did not originate with his own race.

There were, however, others than members of his race who objected to his ideas and activities. These included, in addition to his writings, the act of preaching or leading religious gatherings at Hartford and New Haven, where he had found shelter during the Revolution with other Long Islanders sympathetic to the American cause. Those who objected held that he was not qualified to teach. Qualified or not, however, he asserted he would continue to "endeavour by divine assistance to enlighten the minds" of his brethren, "a poor despised nation, whom God in his wise providence has permitted to be brought from their native place to a Christian land, and many thousands born in what are called Christian families, and brought up to years of understanding."

> Charles A. Vertanes, "Jupiter Hammon: Early Negro Poet of L. I.," *Nassau County Historical Journal* 18, No. 1 (Winter 1957): 12–13

SIDNEY KAPLAN   It is altogether possible that Jupiter Hammon was a preacher to the slaves in the communities of Long Island and Connecticut where he labored for the Lloyds. *An Evening Thought*, an antiphonal poem echoing the word "Salvation" in twenty-three of its eighty-eight lines, has all the ringing ecstatic hope for heavenly freedom with "tender love" that charges the earliest spirituals of the enslaved. The preacher calls and the flock responds—thus the "Penetential Cries."

> Dear Jesus unto Thee we cry,
>   Give us the Preparation;
> Turn not away thy tender Eye;
>   We seek thy true Salvation. . . .
> Lord hear our penetential Cry:
>   Salvation from above;
> It is the Lord that doth supply
>   With his Redeeming Love.

Jupiter Hammon wrote this hymn on Christmas Day of 1760, and for the next forty years, whenever he cried out in print to his black brothers and sisters, his theme, more or less, was always salvation. Yet there are hints towards the end of his career of a certain impatience, a feeling that freedom was possible—and desirable—in the Here as well as in the After.

Sidney Kaplan, *The Black Presence in the Era of the American Revolution 1770–1800* (Washington, DC: New York Graphic Society, 1973), pp. 171, 173

R. RODERICK PALMER   Hammon's best known work is his prose piece "An Address to the Negroes of the State of New York." *Black Poets of the United States*, Jean Wagner's critical commentary, which rightly evaluates Hammon's words to his fellow blacks, declares that today readers can find little to praise in Hammon's religious fervor, which overlaid a strange torpor in his racial sensitivity.

In the first section of the Address entitled "Respecting Obedience to Masters," Hammon says

> Now whether it is right, and lawful, in the sight of God, for them
> to make slaves of us or not, I am certain that while we are slaves,
> it is our duty to obey our masters, in all their lawful commands
> and mind them unless we are bid to do that which we know to be
> sin, or forbidden in God's word.

Similar moral precepts, sentiments, and declarations appear in the second section which delineates the virtues of honesty and faithfulness. Hammon concludes his Address with a few words "to those Negroes who have their liberty" by admonishing them in this vein:

> You have more time to read God's holy word, and to take care of
> the salvation of your souls. Let me beg you to spend your time in
> this way, or it will be better for you if you had always been slaves.
> If you are idle, and take to bad courses, you will hurt those of
> your brethren who are slaves, and do all in your power to prevent
> their being free.

Wagner and other critics appraise such dicta as that of a neophyte who had been carefully indoctrinated by his slave masters and whom kindly treatment had reduced to docility. ⟨. . .⟩

Considering the numbers of blacks who listened to Hammon's preachments, one can vividly envision the leadership he could have exerted in apparent arduous struggles for freedom. A pervasive sense of dissatisfaction with American life for blacks in pre-American Revolutionary days had to have its roots in discontent, protest, and rebellion, even in the North. Not so with Hammon! He was content as a "do-gooder", a religious man who believed in and taught the virtue of obedience to oppressed slaves. I must caution, however, that in evaluating Hammon's religiosity, the critic must not study obvious racial feelings rampant at that time but the religious feelings of Hammon as well. He was thoroughly indoctrinated in the Christian ethic and was truly unable to function otherwise.

> R. Roderick Palmer, "Jupiter Hammon's Poetic Exhortations," *CLA Journal* 18, No. 1 (September 1974): 24–25, 27

EUGENE B. REDMOND   That Hammon himself was deeply religious is reflected in his poetry—as with many black poets, e.g. ⟨Robert⟩ Hayden, today—and he obviously labored under the influence of Methodism and the Wesleyan revival ⟨. . .⟩ In the poem to Phillis Wheatley, he notes that it was through "God's tender mercy" that she was kidnaped from Africa and brought to America as a slave. And Hammon seemed, generally, to reflect the prevailing white attitude toward the "dark" continent: one engulfed in ignorance, barbarism and evil. Obviously not as well read as Phillis Wheatley, Hammon was unable to sustain universal and intellectual levels. Born a slave, he belonged to the influential family of Lloyd's Neck on Long Island and was encouraged by his masters to write and publish poetry. There is not a great deal of information available on the life of Hammon; but it is difficult to understand why such an intelligent black man, who lived such a long life, mirrored almost complete ignorance of the horrors of slavery—despite the daily local newspaper and verbal accounts and discussions of the "peculiar institution."

> Eugene B. Redmond, *Drumvoices: The Mission of Afro-American Poetry* (Garden City, NY: Doubleday/Anchor Books, 1976), p. 52

BLYDEN JACKSON   In his small way ⟨. . .⟩ Hammon was a man of letters, a somewhat dedicated practitioner of the art of literature, as Lucy Terry was not. Because of its historical distinctiveness, "An Evening Thought" has attracted more attention than any of his other works. As poetry it approximates the quality of the poetry in "Bars Fight." It is eighty-eight lines long and affects the ballad stanza as that stanza had been corrupted in the hymns written by the Methodists whose new version of Christian piety had arisen in Hammon's own era. Perhaps more importantly, "An Evening Thought" evinces the seemingly almost absolute sovereignty exercised by Methodism over Hammon's life and thought. One can only conjecture how Hammon, a lowly slave, would have reacted to Calvinism with its aristocratic doctrine of the few and favored elect. But Methodism, through its advocacy of Christ's redeeming grace, offered salvation to everyone, no matter how mean or desperate the state on earth in which that someone had lived. In "An Evening Thought" the very term *salvation* occurs twenty-three times. A crude echolalia haunts the poem. *Jesus* occurs in it nine times; *Lord*, or *God*, fourteen; and there is repeated reference in it to the Holy Word. Perhaps Hammon was enthralled by incantation. It appears far likelier, however, that his obsessive reiteration of certain terms reflects an interest of his not so much in sound as in sense. He lived in a world which was yet to experience the impact of post-Darwinian science. Clearly, an eschatology culminating in a final divine judgment—beyond the grave, of course—whereby saints and sinners would finally receive their due and just rewards permeated at every juncture his reactions to the environment with which he daily dealt. He is consistent in all that he wrote. He addresses Phillis Wheatley to remind her of her good fortune in being brought from savagery to a Christian land and to admonish her to make the most of her possible advantages from such a providential turn in her affairs. His thoughts on death for children are thoughts on damnation and salvation. His kindly master is a Person of the Holy Trinity and is not to be mistaken as a mere human slave owner, like any one, for instance, of the Lloyds. So his dutiful servant is a wise seeker after the peace that passeth all understanding, the blissful peace of angelic immortality. Even when he lectures his fellow Negroes, slaves and free, in the state of New York, it is not so much their lot here as what their lot may be in the hereafter which is his major theme.

Blyden Jackson, *A History of Afro-American Literature* (Baton Rouge: Louisiana University Press, 1989), Vol. 1, pp. 34–35

PHILLIP M. RICHARDS   Hammon's first two sermons, written near the end of the Revolutionary War, show that the politicized Puritanism of the period induced a deep optimism in the slave poet. These works assert that for blacks, moral reformation could yield national deliverance as well as the moral transformation of America and the world. It is, therefore, not surprising that the failure of a millennial society and black freedom to emerge after the Revolution created the same pessimism in Hammon that it did in his white ministerial counterparts. In his final written piece, "An Address to the Negroes of the State of New-York," Hammon echoes the doubts of the ministers who in the late 1780s also expressed their anxieties over the ability of the new America to summon the civic virtue required by a republic. Adopting the stance of Paul reprimanding his Jewish countrymen for failing to adopt Christianity, Hammon laments the wickedness as well as the oppression of his African peers:

> When I am writing to you with a design to say something to you
> for your own good, and with a view to promote your happiness, I
> can with truth and sincerity join with the apostle Paul, when
> speaking of his own nation the Jews, and say: *"that I have great
> heaviness and continual sorrow in my heart for my brethren, my
> kinsmen according to the flesh."* Yes my dear brethren, when I think
> of you, which is very often, and of the poor, despised and
> miserable state you are in, as to the things of this world, and
> when I think of your ignorance and stupidity, and the great
> wickedness of the most of you, I am pained to the heart.

Hammon's pessimism over the failure of a virtuous society to emerge among either blacks or whites led to his adoption of an intensely prophetic stance in which he castigated whites for their immorality and argued, as before, that blacks must exercise autonomous virtue. Furthermore, within the context of an increasingly prophetic stance, Hammon held out the hope of the transformation of American society.

Hammon criticized whites for refusing to give blacks their freedom, an act which should have naturally arisen from the moral reformation advocated by the Whigs. "That liberty is a great thing we may know from our own feelings, and we may likewise judge so from the conduct of the white people in the late war. How much money has been spent, and how many lives have been lost to defend their liberty! I must say that I have hoped that God would open their eyes, when they were so much engaged for liberty, to think of the state of the poor blacks, and to pity us." Hammon's disapproval of whites carries over into a number of implicit criticisms of their morality as well as into explicit exhortations for blacks to act independently of their "superiors," their white masters. The slave preacher exhorts his black audience not to use profanity although the white masters may do so. Hammon counsels his people to read their Bibles although other literate individuals (by implication, whites) do not. And he asserts that blacks must not steal despite the fact that they own nothing—a deprivation which is largely the result of slavery. The upshot of this criticism is that blacks must strive for moral regeneration despite what may be the bad example of their white masters.

Furthermore, Hammon argues that the blacks' very social inferiority to whites—in terms of ignorance and poverty—may make them better fitted for redemption and moral regeneration. "There are some things very encouraging in God's word for such ignorant creatures as we are; for God hath not chosen the rich of this world. Not many rich, not many noble are called, but God hath chosen the weak things of this world, and things which are not, to confound the things that are." Considering Hammon's accounts of black wretchedness and his exhortations for moral autonomy, his appropriation of biblical rhetoric is suggestive. It contains a hint that blacks will change their social reality—"confound things that are"—because of their moral and spiritual strengths. Hammon thereby implies that blacks can through these strengths persuade whites to abolish slavery. And this implication lies behind Hammon's sharp criticism of those free blacks who do not become useful members of society: "now all those of you who follow any bad courses, and who do not take care to get an honest living by your labour and industry, are doing more to prevent our being free than any-body else." ⟨. . .⟩

At the core of Hammon's call for moral reformation was the notion that as God's chosen people, blacks must uphold the covenant to preserve their status as a nation. As Harry S. Stout has recently shown, calls to uphold the covenant formed a staple of much Congregational preaching during the Revolutionary period. However, an important distinction exists between the white political preaching studied by Stout and Hammon's sermons. Whig Congregationalist preaching on the covenant was often infused with libertarian themes, themes which are conspicuously absent in Hammon's covenantal rhetoric. Ministers insisted that "in entering into his covenant with New England, God simultaneously provided a place of liberty, which had to be maintained or the covenant would be annulled" ⟨Stout⟩. For the rebelling colonists, liberty was maintained at present in order to keep covenant privileges. On the contrary, Hammon clearly looked ahead to the future, the end of the war, as a time of the fulfillment of covenant promises of freedom for blacks. And although he advocated manumission in his final oration, he did not propose either petitioning or revolution as a means of emancipation in the present. Instead, piety, a moral walk, and prayer were the chosen means of bringing about the completion of the covenant plan. There are reasons for Hammon's gradualist stance. He was a slave speaking to other slaves as well as free blacks. During the Revolutionary period, the open advocacy of immediate manumission would be inflammatory. Given his rhetorical context, he could not publicly rouse the black nation and attack slavery. More importantly, the concern of his rhetoric was with the preparation of his community for freedom. Hammon's calls for moral reformation and his use of the jeremiads were means of collective socialization that sought to prepare blacks (and whites) for life within American society.

Phillip M. Richards, "Nationalist Themes in the Preaching of Jupiter Hammon," *Early American Literature* 25, No. 2 (1990): 132–34

◈ *Bibliography*

An Evening Thought: Salvation by Christ, with Penetential Cries. 1760.

An Address to Miss Phillis Wheatly, Ethiopian Poetess, in Boston. 1778.

An Essay on the Ten Virgins. 1779. Lost.

A Winter Piece: Being a Series Exhortation, with a Call to the Unconverted; and a Short Contemplation on the Death of Jesus Christ. 1782.

An Evening's Improvement: Shewing, the Necessity of Beholding the Lamb of God; to Which Is Added, A Dialogue, Entitled, The Kind Master and Dutiful Servant. 1783.

An Address to the Negroes in the State of New-York. 1787.

America's First Negro Poet: The Complete Works of Jupiter Hammon of Long Island. Ed. Stanley Austin Ransom, Jr. 1970.

Frances E. W. Harper
c. 1825–1911

FRANCES ELLEN WATKINS HARPER, civil rights leader, abolitionist, suffragette, and poet, was born in Baltimore, Maryland, most probably in 1825, although some records indicate it may have been 1824. Although Maryland was a slave state at the time, Harper was born free to free parents. Her mother died when she was three or four years of age, and Harper moved in with her aunt, attending a school for free blacks owned by her uncle. Her formal education ended when she reached her teens, but she took a position in a Baltimore bookstore and used the opportunity to read widely.

Harper's first volume of poetry, *Forest Leaves,* was probably published in 1845. No copies of the book exist today, but it is thought that Harper republished the poems that appeared in it in later poetry collections. In 1850, wishing to move to a free state, Harper took a position at Union Seminary, a new school for free blacks founded by the African Methodist Episcopal Church and located near Columbus, Ohio. Harper did not enjoy teaching and wanted to be more directly involved in social activism. She moved to Little York, Pennsylvania, a town on the Underground Railroad, where she met and was deeply influenced by abolitionist and orator William Grant Still.

In 1853 Harper relinquished her teaching position, and in 1854 published her successful *Poems on Miscellaneous Subjects* (with a preface by William Lloyd Garrison) and gave her first abolitionist lecture. She became a professional lecturer for the abolitionist movement and was supported by various antislavery societies as she traveled from town to town, lecturing and reading her poems. Her poetry, not surprisingly, is written in an oral style and uses biblical themes and imagery familiar to her nineteenth-century audience. Harper created lyrical and emotional poems while maintaining the formal construction of the rhymed quatrain.

In 1860 she married Fenton Harper, a widower from Cincinnati, settled on a farm near Columbus, and had a daughter named Mary. Fenton Harper died in 1864, and Frances Harper resumed lecturing and toured the South twice between 1867 and 1871. She published *Moses: A Story of the Nile* in 1869, *Poems* in 1871, and *Sketches of Southern Life* in 1872. *Moses*, a blank verse biblical allegory without overt racial references, is considered by many critics to be her best work.

Harper became increasingly involved with the woman's suffrage movement and was especially concerned with the condition of newly freed black women in the Reconstruction South. In 1892 she published her only novel, *Iola Leroy; or, Shadows Uplifted*, a story about a mulatto and her family during and after the Civil War. The novel has recently attracted a great deal of critical attention, mostly focused on Harper's treatment of her title character, the mulatto Iola. Frances Harper died of heart failure on February 22, 1911.

◈ *Critical Extracts*

WILLIAM STILL   Fifty thousand copies at least of ⟨Harper's⟩ four small books have been sold to those who have listened to her eloquent lectures. One of those productions entitled *Moses* has been used to entertain audiences with evening readings in various parts of the country. With what effect may be seen from the two brief notices as follows:

> "Mrs. F. E. W. Harper delivered a poem upon 'Moses' in Wilbraham to a large and delighted audience. She is a woman of high moral tone, with superior native powers highly cultivated, and a captivating eloquence that holds her audience in rapt attention from the beginning to the close. She will delight any intelligent audience, and those who wish first-class lecturers cannot do better than to secure her services."—*Zion's Herald, Boston*
>
> "Mrs Frances E. W. Harper read her poem of 'Moses' last evening at Rev. Mr. Harrison's church to a good audience. It deals with the story of the Hebrew Moses from his finding in the wicker basket on the Nile to his death on Mount Nebo and his burial in an unknown grave; following closely the Scripture account. It contains about 700 lines, beginning with blank verse of the common measure, and changing to other measures, but always without rhyme; and is a pathetic and well-sustained piece. Mrs. Harper recited it with good effect, and it was well received. She is a lady of much talent, and always speaks well, particularly

when her subject related to the condition of her own people, in whose welfare, before and since the war, she has taken the deepest interest. As a lecturer Mrs. Harper is more effective than most of those who come before our lyceums; with a natural eloquence that is very moving."—*Galesburgh Register, Ill.*

Grace Greenwood, in the *Independent* in noticing a Course of Lectures in which Mrs. Harper spoke (in Philadelphia) pays this tribute to her:

> Next on the course was Mrs Harper, a colored woman; about as colored as some of the Cuban belles I have met with at Saratoga. She has a noble head, this bronze muse; a strong face, with a shadowed glow upon it, indicative of thoughtful fervor, and of a nature most femininely sensitive, but not in the least morbid. Her form is delicate, her hands daintily small. She stands quietly beside her desk, and speaks without notes, with gestures few and fitting. Her manner is marked by dignity and composure. She is never assuming, never theatrical. In the first part of her lecture she was most impressive in her pleading for the race with whom her lot is cast. There was something touching in her attitude as their representative. The woe of two hundred years sighed through her tones. Every glance of her sad eyes was a mournful remonstrance against injustice and wrong. Feeling on her soul, as she must have felt it, the chilling weight of caste, she seemed to say:
>
> > I lift my heavy heart up solemnly,
> > As once Electra her sepulchral urn.
>
> . . . As I listened to her, there swept over me, in a chill wave of horror, the realization that this noble woman had she not been rescued from her mother's condition, might have been sold on the auction-block, to the highest bidder—her intellect, fancy, eloquence, the flashing wit, that might make the delight of a Parisian saloon, and her pure, Christian character all thrown in— the recollection that women like her could be dragged out of public conveyances in our own city, or frowned out of fashionable churches by Anglo-Saxon saints.

William Still, "Frances Ellen Watkins Harper," *The Underground Rail Road*, rev. ed. (Philadelphia: People's Publishing, 1871), pp. 779–80

ROBERT T. KERLIN   Mrs. Harper attained to a greater popularity than any poet of her race prior to Dunbar. As many as ten thousand copies of some of her poems were in circulation in the middle of the last century.

Her success was not unmerited. Many singers of no greater merit have enjoyed greater celebrity. She was thoroughly in the fashion of her times, as Phillis Wheatley was in the yet prevalent fashion of Pope, or, perhaps more accurately, Cowper. The models in the middle of the nineteenth century were Mrs. Hemans, Whittier, and Longfellow. It is in their manner she writes. A serene and beautiful Christian spirit tells a moral tale in fluent ballad stanzas, not without poetic phrasing. In all she beholds, in all she experiences, there is a lesson. There is no grief without consolation. Serene resignation breathes through all her poems—at least through those written after her freedom was achieved.

> Robert T. Kerlin, "The Heritage of Song," *Negro Poets and Their Poems* (Washington, DC: Associated Publishers, 1923), pp. 26–27

VERNON LOGGINS   *Sketches of Southern Life*, originally published in 1872, and reprinted, each time with additions, in 1888 and 1896, presents in a connected series of poems two characters whom one remembers, Aunt Chloe and Uncle Jacob. Aunt Chloe is the narrator, and a very rambling one. While she does not speak in dialect, her idiom is true to the life of the primitive Negro. She says in "The Deliverance," in describing the conduct of the slaves on her plantation when they hear that they are free:

> We just laughed, and danced, and shouted,
>   And prayed, and sang, and cried,
> And we thought dear Uncle Jacob
>   Would fairly crack his side.

She has a homely Negro wit that sees straight through the farce of the black man in national politics, and her vigorous comment on Johnson and Grant is a charming display of honest common sense. One regrets that *Sketches of Southern Life* contains pieces, mainly on reform topics, in which Aunt Chloe is not the narrator and in which Uncle Jacob, a pleasing old mystic, is not on hand to warn and exhort. In creating these two characters Mrs. Harper perhaps did more than any other Negro poet before Dunbar in getting close to the reality of primitive Negro life.

However, in her most consistently even piece of work, that which shows her highest achievement as a versifier, she has nothing to say about the Negro. It is *Moses: a Story of the Nile*, published as early as 1869. The poem was obviously written to be read in public, and the opening hints that Mrs. Harper might have intended to make of it a drama. In a scene, the setting for which the reader is left to construct for himself, Moses discloses to the

Princess who has reared him his determination to lead his people out of
Egypt. She at first protests, but because she loves Moses as though he were
her own child she finally agrees to his departure. After this opening the
dramatic form is dropped, and the rest of the poem is a straight narrative
of the life adventures of Moses. The verse, often metrically uneven, is the
most natural which Mrs. Harper produced. In passages admitting of pretti-
ness, as in the description of how angels come down from heaven and bury
Moses, there is a delicate charm:

> And when the grave was finished,
> They trod with golden sandals
> Above the sacred spot,
> And the brightest, fairest flowers
> Sprang up beneath their tread.
> Nor broken turf, nor hillock,
> Did e'er reveal that grave,
> And truthful lips have never said,
> "We know where he is laid."

The poem is significant in Negro literature because one who reads it is not
constantly aware of imitation. Mrs. Harper must yield place to Albery A.
Whitman as the most talented Negro poet between Phillis Wheatley and
Paul Laurence Dunbar. But of all Dunbar's predecessors who were not
primitive and spontaneous singers Mrs. Harper came nearest to producing
a fairly extensive body of verse which has a certain originality.

Vernon Loggins, *The Negro Author: His Development in America* (New York: Columbia
University Press, 1931), pp. 343–44

J. SAUNDERS REDDING   In 1854, while Douglass was climbing
in importance as the spokesman and ideal of the Negro race, there appeared
in Philadelphia a thin volume called *Poems on Miscellaneous Subjects,* by
Frances Ellen Watkins. The title is significant, for it indicates a different
trend in the creative urge of the Negro. Except for Jupiter Hammon and
Phillis Wheatley, Negro writers up to this time were interested mainly in
the one theme of slavery and in the one purpose of bringing about freedom.
The treatment of their material was doctrinal, definitely conditioned to the
ends of propaganda. A willful (and perhaps necessary) monopticism had
blinded them to other treatment and to the possibilities in other subjects.
It remained for Miss Watkins, with the implications in the title of her
volume, to attempt a redirection. ⟨. . .⟩

In 1861 Mrs. Harper (Frances Ellen Watkins) wrote to Thomas Hamilton, the editor of the *Anglo-African*, a monthly journal that had been established the year before: "If our talents are to be recognized we must write less of issues that are particular and more of feelings that are general. We are blessed with hearts and brains that compass more than ourselves in our present plight. . . . We must look to the future which, God willing, will be better than the present or the past, and delve into the heart of the world." ⟨. . .⟩

To what degree Frances Ellen Watkins followed her own advice can be judged from her writings. In one sense she was a trail blazer, hacking, however ineffectually, at the dense forest of propaganda and striving to "write less of issues that were particular and more of feelings that were general." But she was seriously limited by the nature and method of her appeal. Immensely popular as a reader ("elocutionist"), the demands of her audience for the sentimental treatment of the old subjects sometimes overwhelmed her. On the occasions when she was free "to delve into the heart of the world" she was apt to gush with pathetic sentimentality over such subjects as wronged innocence, the evils of strong drink, and the blessed state of childhood. ⟨. . .⟩

Practically all the social evils from the double standard of sex morality to corruption in politics were lashed with the scourge of her resentment. Her treatment of these topics never varied: she traced the effects of the evil upon some innocent—a young and dying girl, as in "A Little Child Shall Lead Them," or a virtuous woman, as in "The Double Standard," or a sainted mother, as in "Nothing and Something." But her treating these evils at all entitles her to respect and gratitude as one who created other aims and provided new channels for the creative energies of Negro writers.

In some of Miss Watkins's verse one thing more is to be noted especially. In the volume called *Sketches of Southern Life* the language she puts in the mouths of Negro characters has a fine racy, colloquial tang. In these poems she managed to hurdle a barrier by which Dunbar was later to feel himself tripped. The language is not dialect. She retained the speech patterns of Negro dialect, thereby giving herself greater emotional scope (had she wished or had the power to use it) than the humorous and the pathetic to which it is generally acknowledged dialect limits one. In all of her verse Miss Watkins attempted to suit her language to her theme. In *Moses* she gives her language a certain solemnity and elevation of tone. In her pieces on slavery she employs short, teethy, angry monosyllables. Her use of dialectal patterns was no accident. She anticipated James Weldon Johnson.

J. Saunders Redding, *To Make a Poet Black* (Chapel Hill: University of North Carolina Press, 1939), pp. 38–43

PATRICIA LIGGINS HILL   Harper's popularity ⟨. . .⟩ is not based
on conventional notions of poetic excellence. In her handling of poetic
forms and her major subject matter—race (abolition in particular), religion,
and women's rights—she is considered generally to be less a technician
than either of her contemporary abolitionist poets, James Whitfield and
George Moses Horton. ⟨. . .⟩ With the exception of *Moses: A Story of the
Nile* (1869) and *Sketches of Southern Life* (1872), Harper's poetry varies little
in form, language, and poetic technique.

Harper's fame as a poet, instead, rests on her excellent skills in oral poetry
delivery. ⟨. . .⟩

Indeed, there are similarities between Frances Harper's poetry and the
verse of the new black poets—Imamu Baraka (LeRoi Jones), Madhubuti
(Don L. Lee), Nikki Giovanni, Lalia Mannan (Sonia Sanchez), and others.
Just as these latter-day poets base their oral protest poetry primarily on
direct imagery, simple diction, and the rhythmic language of the street to
reach the masses of black people, Harper relies on vivid, striking imagery,
simplistic language, and the musical quality and form of the ballad to appeal
to large masses of people, black and white, for her social protest. Moreover,
she, like the new black poets, embraces an "art for people's sake" aesthetic,
rather than a Western Caucasian aesthetic assumption, "an art for art's
sake" principle. In her poem "Songs for the People" which is her closest
statement on aesthetics, Harper makes this point clear:

> Let me make the songs for the people,
>   Songs for the old and young;
> Songs to stir like a battle cry
>   Whenever they are sung.
>
> Let me make the songs for the weary,
>   Amid life's fever and fret,
> Till hearts shall relax their tension
>   And careworn brows forget.
>
> I will sing for the poor and aged,
>   When shadows dim their sight,
> Of the bright and restful mansions,
>   Where there shall be no right.
>
> Our world, so worn and weary
>   Needs music, pure and strong
> To hush the jangle and discords
>   Of sorrow, pain and wrong.

Clearly, in this poem and in her other works, Harper assumes the stance
of a poet-priestess whose "pure and strong" songs serve to uplift the oppressed

in particular and humanity as a whole. The corpus of her poetry indicates
that she, like the new black poets, however, is primarily concerned with
uplifting the masses of black people. According to William Still the question
as to how Harper could best serve her race lay at the very core of her literary
and professional career. She answers this question early in her career when
she writes to Still in 1853 that she has decided to devote her life to the
liberation of her people. As she expresses to him, "It may be that God
Himself has written upon both my heart and brain a commissary to use
time, talent, and energy in the cause of freedom." This intrinsic concern
for black liberation led her to envision herself as a race-builder, the black
shepherd who will provide leadership for her flock of sheep (the black
masses). In her February 1870 letter to Still, Harper states, "I am standing
with my race on the threshhold ⟨sic⟩ of a new era . . . and yet today, with
my limited and fragmented knowledge, I may help my race forward a little.
Some of our people remind me of sheep without a shepherd."

> Patricia Liggins Hill, " 'Let Me Make the Songs for the People': A Study of Frances
> Watkins Harper's Poetry," *Black American Literature Forum* 15, No. 1 (Spring 1981):
> 60

FARAH JASMINE GRIFFIN   Much in ⟨Harper's⟩ discourse foreshadows that of Booker T. Washington, yet there is a sense that Harper,
because she lives and identifies with the people, begins to be more concerned
with their day-to-day survival. If as ⟨August⟩ Meier points out, the concerns
of the masses were the acquisition of land, education, and political rights,
Harper's concerns are closely aligned with theirs. She identifies the freedman's landlessness as his biggest problem, then his ignorance and finally
his economic powerlessness. She mentions nothing of political rights.

If Harper differed from other educated, middle-class leaders in her identification of goals for the freedmen, her concerns differed in another very
important aspect also: Hers is the voice that emerges regarding the condition
of Black freedmen. She not only speaks to them, but goes on to represent
their concerns to whites and northern Blacks through articles and poems.
In a letter to Still she writes:

> Part of my lectures are given privately to women and for them
> I never make any charge or take up any collection. I am now
> going to have a private meeting with the women of this place. I
> am going to talk to them about their daughters and about things
> connected with the welfare of the race. Now is the time for our
> women to begin to plant the roots of progress under the
> hearthstone.

Harper's notion that reform begins at home emerges from two different but significant themes. She is certainly influenced by the 19th century cult of domesticity that stressed the role of women as mothers and wives. However, Harper is also calling on what historian Jacqueline Jones (1986) has identified as the subversive nature of Black women's roles within their families.

Harper sees Black women, though denied political enfranchisement, as the bearers of values, stability and strength in their home lives. By doing this they subvert the intentions of white patriarchal society to keep Blacks in subordinate positions and strip them of all sense of power. Nowhere is this theme more evident than in Harper's poem "Deliverance."

Though the poem is full of stereotypes suggesting matriarchal women and ignorant, easily led Black men, it depicts Black women as politically enlightened and though disenfranchised, politically powerful in their roles as wives and mothers:

> But when John Thomas Reder brought
> His wife some flour and meat,
> And told her he had sold his vote
> For something good to eat,
>
> You ought to see Aunt Kitty raise
> And head her blaze away;
> She gave the meat and flour a toss
> And said they should not stay . . .
>
> You'd laugh to see Lucinda Grange
> Upon her husband's track
> When he sold his vote for rations
> She made him take 'em back
>
> Day after day did Milly Green
> Just follow after Joe,
> And told him if he voted wrong
> To take his rags and go.
>
> I think Curnel Johnson said
> His side had won the day
> Had not we women radicals
> Just got right in the way.

Despite the offensive stereotypes of the poem, many of Harper's concepts are steeped in the reality of the South. The women are strong, politically enlightened and in control of their homes, through which they influence society.

In an article entitled "Colored Women of the South" and published in the January 1878 issue of the *Englishwoman's Review*, Harper provides factual accounts of individual Black women who make education possible, and who have gained significant business experience, been successful at farming ventures as well as organizing themselves for the good of their communities:

> They do a double duty, a man's share in the field and a woman's
> part at home, when the men lose their work through political
> affiliations, the women stand by them and say "stand by your
> principles," by organized effort, colored women have been able to
> help each other in sickness and provide respectable funerals for
> the dead.

The women emerge from the articles not as the henpecking matriarchs of the poems, but instead as very human wives and mothers who are supportive of their husbands and who maintain a sense of community through their mutual aid activities. In this sense they are "women radicals."

Farah Jasmine Griffin, "Frances Ellen Watkins Harper in the Reconstruction South,"
SAGE: A Scholarly Journal on Black Women, Student Supplement 1988, p. 46

DEBORAH E. McDOWELL   Although ⟨the Victorian⟩ ideology of domesticity was the veritable antithesis of the black woman's reality, Harper, like the majority of black writers of her era—both men and women—ironically accommodated her "new" model image of black womanhood to its contours. ⟨. . .⟩ The image of the Lady combined and conflated physical appearance with character traits. Immortalized particularly in the southern antebellum novel, the image required "physical beauty [i.e. fair skin] . . . fragility, refinement and helplessness." "The closest black women could come to such an ideal, at least physically," ⟨Barbara⟩ Christian continues, "would . . . have to be the mulatta, quadroon, or octoroon." Iola ⟨in *Iola Leroy*⟩ fulfills this physical requirement. "My! but she's putty," says the slave through whose eyes we first see her. "Beautiful long hair comes way down her back; putty blue eyes, an' jis' ez white ez anybody's in dis place." ⟨. . .⟩

By giving Iola a role to play in the larger struggle for racial uplift, Harper modified the image of the southern lady, but it is important to note that Iola's role in the struggle is enacted within the boundaries of the traditional expectations of women as mothers and nurturers, expectations that form the cornerstone of the cult of true womanhood. According to Iola, "a great amount of sin and misery springs from the weakness and inefficiency of women." In "The Education of Mothers," one of the two public speeches she gives in the novel (public speaking being largely reserved for men in the text), she appeals for "a union of women with the warmest hearts and clearest brains to help in the moral education of the race." ⟨. . .⟩

In the course of *Iola Leroy*, as Iola fulfills her role as exemplary black woman she comes to resemble a human being less and less and a saint more and more. We learn very little about her thoughts, her inner life. Nothing about her is individualized, nor does this seem to be Harper's chief concern, for she is creating an exemplary type who is always part of some larger framework. ⟨. . .⟩ Every detail of Iola's life, down to the most personal experiences of family life, is stripped of its intimate implications and invested with social and mythical implications. It is significant that of all the Old Testament types, she identifies with Moses and Nehemiah, for "they were willing to put aside their own advantages for their race and country."

Iola's role as social and moral exemplar is paralleled by the novel's role as exemplum. Like its title character, *Iola Leroy* is on trial before the world. It aims for a favorable verdict by choosing its models carefully. Harper's most visible model is Harriet Beecher Stowe's *Uncle Tom's Cabin*, the most popular novel of the mid-nineteenth century in America. ⟨. . .⟩

Harper's choice of *Uncle Tom's Cabin* as a model is a logical and appropriate one, given the polemical and public role that she expected her novel to play, a role that Stowe's novel had played to unrivaled success with an audience comprised mainly of northern white Christians. Harper addresses and appeals to this audience directly in the afternote of the novel: "From threads of fact and fiction I have woven a story whose mission will not be in vain if it awaken in the hearts of our countrymen a stronger sense of justice and a more Christlike humanity in behalf of those whom the fortunes of war threw, homeless, ignorant and poor, upon the threshold of a new era." Those northern whites might be more inclined to lend their assistance to this homeless and displaced lot if the images of black life that Harper and her black contemporaries valued and affirmed accorded with that audience's horizon of social and literary expectations. In this respect, *Iola Leroy* is in company with a number of novels by black writers of its era, all dedicated to a public mission, all foundering on the shoals of two contradictory attempts: "to conform to the accepted social [and] literary . . . standards of their day and their almost antithetical need to portray their own people with honesty and imagination" ⟨Arlene Elder⟩.

    Deborah E. McDowell, " 'The Changing Same': Generation Connections and Black Women Novelists," *New Literary History* 18, No. 2 (Winter 1987): 284–85

ELIZABETH YOUNG   ⟨. . .⟩ Frances Harper's 1892 novel, *Iola Leroy; or, Shadows Uplifted*, offers a powerful vision of the Civil War years as seen by this prominent activist for black rights, feminism, and temperance. At sixty-seven, Frances Ellen Watkins Harper was an experienced lecturer, essayist, short-story writer, and poet when her only novel was published. *Iola Leroy* is the story of a woman, the novel's eponymous heroine, raised as a privileged white daughter of the antebellum South who discovers on the eve of the Civil War that she is of mixed-race ancestry, and who is then sold into slavery. Rescued by the Union army, she eventually reunites with her family when the war is over. Black feminist criticism has recently brought new attention to *Iola Leroy*. Hazel Carby, for example, argues in a persuasive reading of the novel that Iola's journey from orphaned youth to family-filled adulthood both recalls the mid-nineteenth-century domestic "woman's novel" and recasts its plot in the context of the black family. Iola's triumphant claim of family at novel's end applies "not only to the individual heroine but also to the entire race," for it serves, Carby argues, as the vehicle for Harper's observations on the black diaspora and the emerging postwar role of black intellectuals.

We may take the politics of domesticity in another direction, however, by viewing *Iola Leroy* as a domestic novel about a domestic political crisis: the Civil War. Far beyond simply supplying a prelude to the novel's Reconstruction plot, the war profoundly affects the novel's formal and thematic concerns. As a reading of history, *Iola Leroy* rewrites the conventions of war narrative, foregrounding black heroism in combat. Black women are central to this effort, not only as wartime actors but also as mothers whose presence in the narrative frames its war sections. Indeed, Harper embeds the war in a narrative trajectory of maternal quest and reunion, simultaneously feminizing war narrative and using this literary form to represent the importance of maternal and familial structures in the black community.

This use of the Civil War, intercutting the axes of race and gender, is also specific to its meaning as an *internal* conflict. Harper uses "civil war" as a metaphor to describe a variety of conflicts outside the formal battlefield, among them Iola's resistance to the dynamics of interracial rape and her decision, as a light-skinned mulatta, not to pass for white. Engaging and interweaving a variety of antinomies—black/white, male/female, North/South—Harper shows individual identity to be decisively marked by both gender and race. The formations of war, in other words, serve in *Iola Leroy* as a model for the construction of subjectivity.

What complicates this portrayal further is that by the time Harper wrote the novel, the Civil War had already been structured by literary conventions as a series of novelistic plots about sexuality and marriage. Reading Harper's novel against D. W. Griffith's overtly racist 1915 film *The Birth of a Nation*—which elaborates and epitomizes these conventions—suggests the extent to which metaphor determined the politic of Civil War discourse and, consequently, the extent to which Harper's use of metaphor acts as a strategic political intervention. That is, the novel's use of metaphor is reciprocal: *Iola Leroy* simultaneously employs the war as a metaphor for identity and offers a novelistic plot of individual identity that metaphorically restages the Civil War itself. *Iola Leroy*, in short, sets race and gender at battle with war, history at war with metaphor, and representation—political and literary—in conflict with itself.

> Elizabeth Young, "Warring Fictions: *Iola Leroy* and the Color of Gender," *American Literature* 64, No. 2 (June 1992): 273–75

❖ *Bibliography*

Forest Leaves. c. 1845. Lost.

Poems on Miscellaneous Subjects. 1854, 1855.

Poems on Miscellaneous Subjects: Second Series. 1855.

Moses: A Story of the Nile. 1869, 1889.

Poems. 1871.

Sketches of Southern Life. 1872, 1887.

Achan's Sin. c. 1875.

The Sparrow's Fall and Other Poems. c. 1890.

Enlightened Motherhood. 1892.

Iola Leroy; or, Shadows Uplifted. 1892.

The Martyr of Alabama and Other Poems. c. 1894.

Atlanta Offering: Poems. 1895.

Light Beyond the Darkness. c. 1895.

Poems. 1895, 1900.

Idylls of the Bible. 1901.

Complete Poems. Ed. Maryemma Graham. 1988.

A Brighter Coming Day: A Frances Ellen Watkins Harper Reader. Ed. Frances Smith Foster. 1990.

George Moses Horton
c. 1797–c. 1883

GEORGE MOSES HORTON was born in slavery on the farm of William Horton in Northampton County, North Carolina. The year of his birth is probably 1797, as he states in *The Hope of Liberty* (1829) that he was thirty-two years old. Little is known of Horton's parents; Horton himself says that his mother was forced to leave her husband when Horton was still a boy, and this separation may have been a result of William Horton's transferral of his farm to Chatham County, near Chapel Hill, in 1800. Nevertheless, it was at this time that Horton began gaining a rudimentary education from Wesleyan hymnals and remnants of schoolbooks obtained from white children. Although Horton did not learn to write until years later, as an adolescent he was already composing poems and committing them to memory.

In 1814 Horton became the property of William Horton's son James. At some point during the next five years he became a fruit vendor in the Chapel Hill area, where he met students from the university and recited his poetry for them. The students began asking Horton to write acrostics and love-poems for their girlfriends, paying him fifty or seventy-five cents for each poem. Horton claims to have written dozens of such poems for young men in Virginia, South Carolina, and Georgia, but only a few survive. The young men also gave Horton books—including the works of Shakespeare, Milton, Byron, and other poets who would influence Horton's later poetry.

At Chapel Hill Horton also met Caroline Lee Hentz, a poet and novelist who lent him assistance with his work and transcribed some of his poetry. In 1828 she arranged for the publication of two of Horton's poems in a newspaper, the *Lancaster* (Mass.) *Gazette*. At this time Horton was befriended by many abolitionists, who attempted unsuccessfully in 1828 and 1829 to purchase his freedom. Horton's collection of poems, *The Hope of Liberty*, was published by these abolitionists in the hope of raising enough money to give James Horton the sum he required to liberate Horton. This effort failed, as the book sold few copies; but it constituted the first book published by a slave in a southern state. In 1837 the volume was reprinted as *Poems by a Slave*.

In 1830 the North Carolina legislature passed a law declaring it illegal to teach blacks how to read or write. Nevertheless, Horton's local reputation as a poet flourished as he continued writing poems for Chapel Hill students. At some time in the 1830s or 1840s Horton married a slave woman from the farm of Franklin Snipes; they had at least one son and one daughter. In 1843 two of his poems, including the "Ode to Liberty," appeared in the *Southern Literary Messenger*. Two years later his *Poetical Works* was issued, but it seems by design to have been purged of any inflammatory material. Although Horton wrote a lengthy autobiographical preface to the volume, he does not seem to have had much say in its selection or publication. The book's publisher, Dennis Heartt, speaks of a previous volume of Horton's entitled *The Museum*, but it is not clear whether it was ever published; if it was, no copies are known to survive.

At the outbreak of the Civil War Horton fled to Raleigh, where a contingent of Union troops was stationed. There he met Captain Will H. S. Banks, a cavalry officer from Michigan. As the war was ending Banks arranged for the publication of a large volume of Horton's poetry entitled *Naked Genius*. The book was not successful and failed to bring about the publication of another volume, *The Black Poet*, advertised at the back of *Naked Genius*.

After the war Horton, now free, settled in Philadelphia. He seems to have continued to write—Collier Cobb, a professor at the University of North Carolina, reports visiting Horton late in life and hearing that he was writing short stories based on legends from the Bible—but no further volumes of his work appeared. Horton is thought to have died around 1883, but the exact date and place of his death are uncertain.

▓ *Critical Extracts*

UNSIGNED   George, who is the author of the following Poetical effusions, is a Slave, the property of Mr. James Horton, of Chatham County, North Carolina. He has been in the habit, some years past, of producing poetical pieces, sometimes on suggested subjects, to such persons as would write them while he dictated. Several compositions of his have already appeared in the Raleigh Register. Some have made their way into the Boston

Newspapers, and have evoked expressions of approbation and surprise. Many persons have now become much interested in the promotion of his prospects, some of whom are elevated in office and literary attainments. They are solicitous that efforts at length be made to obtain by subscription, a sum sufficient for his emancipation, upon the condition of his going in the vessel which shall first afterwards sail for Liberia. It is his earnest and only wish to become a member of that Colony, to enjoy its privileges, and apply his industry and mental abilities to the promotion of its prospects and his own. It is upon these terms alone, that the efforts of those who befriend his views are intended to have a final effect.

To put to trial the plan here urged in his behalf, the paper now exhibited is published. Several of his productions are contained in the succeeding pages. Many more might have been added, which would have swelled into a larger size. They would doubtless be interesting to many, but it is hoped that the specimens here inserted will be sufficient to accomplish the object of the publication. Expense will thus be avoided, and the money better employed in enlarging the sum applicable for his emancipation.—It is proposed, that in every town or vicinity where contributions are made, they may be put into the hands of some person, who will humanely consent to receive them, and give notice to Mr. Weston R. Gales, in Raleigh, of the amount collected. As soon as it is ascertained that the collections will accomplish the object, it is expected that they will be transmitted without delay to Mr. Weston R. Gales. But should they ultimately prove insufficient, they will be returned to subscribers.

None will imagine it possible that pieces produced as these have been, should be free from blemish in composition or taste. The author is now 32 years of age, and has always laboured in the field on his master's farm, promiscuously with the few others which Mr. Horton owns, in circumstances of the greatest possible simplicity. His master says he knows nothing of his poetry but as he heard of it from others. George knows how to read, and is now learning to write. All his pieces are written down by others; and his reading, which is done at night, and at the usual intervals allowed to slaves, has been much employed on poetry, such as he could procure, this being the species of composition most interesting to him. It is thought best to print his productions without correction, that the mind of the reader may be in no uncertainty as to the originality and genuineness of every part. We shall conclude this account of George, with an assurance that he has been ever a faithful, honest and industrious slave. That his heart has felt deeply and sensitively in this lowest possible condition of human nature, will easily be believed, and is impressively confirmed by one of his stanzas.

Come, melting Pity, from afar,
And break this vast enormous bar
    Between a wretch and thee;
Purchase a few short days of time
And bid the vassal soar sublime,
    On wings of Liberty.

Unsigned, "Explanation," *The Hope of Liberty: Containing a Number of Poetical Pieces*
by George Moses Horton (Raleigh, NC: J. Gales & Son, 1829)

COLLIER COBB   A slave who owned his master; a poet ignorant
of the rules of prosody; a man of letters before he had learned to read; a
writer of short stories who published in several papers simultaneously before
the day of newspaper syndicates; an author who supported himself and his
family in an intellectual center before authorship had attained to the dignity
of a profession in America: such was George Horton, a negro, born in North
Carolina, in 1798.

Like all the members of his race, he was fond of melody and devoted to
church going; and to this religious impulse he owed the cultivation of a
poetic temperament, and the opportunity to study the structure of the short
story.

My attention was drawn to his work several years ago by some verses of
his written for a lady's album in 1840, to the authorship of which he had
relinquished all claim for twenty-five cents. The quality of the verse and
the story of its author led me to look into the man's history and to search
for his work in the files of the newspapers of his day.

George was the property of Mr. James Horton, of Chatham County. He
was a full-blooded black man, something like the type known today as
negroid, yet more Aryan than Semitic in features, and more like the natives
of India and Northern Africa, than the negro south of the Sahara. He
himself, Othello like, boasted of the purity of his black blood. Such is the
description I get of his personal appearance from old residents of Chapel
Hill, who knew him in his prime. ⟨. . .⟩

It was in Philadelphia that he developed his gift of story telling, his
stories being modelled on the old stories of the East, as he had learned them
from his Bible and in many cases being bodily taken from the Scriptures
and made modern as to names and places. In this he was even more successful
than was Benjamin Franklin in his famous paraphrase of the Book of Job.
The source of Horton's inspiration was always hid from any but the closest

students of Holy Writ, and even they did not often recognize their old friends in modern dress.

Collier Cobb, "An American Man of Letters," *University of North Carolina Magazine* 40, No. 1 (October 1909): 3–4, 10

BENJAMIN BRAWLEY   Horton's work showed readily the influence of his models. He used especially the meter of the common evangelical hymns, and cultivated the vague personification of the poets of the eighteenth century. He himself, however, was essentially a romantic poet, as was evinced by his fondness for Byron and Marlowe. His common style is represented by the following lines from his poem entitled "On the Evening and Morning":

> When Evening bids the Sun to rest retire,
> Unwearied Ether sets her lamps on fire;
> Lit by one torch, each is supplied in turn,
> Till all the candles in the concave burn.
> ....
> At length the silver queen begins to rise,
> And spread her glowing mantle in the skies,
> And from the smiling chambers of the east,
> Invites the eye to her resplendent feast.

The passion in the heart of this man, his undoubted gifts as a poet, and the bitter disappointment of his yearnings have all but added one more to the long list of those who died with their ambitions blasted and their most ardent hopes defeated.

Benjamin Brawley, "Three Negro Poets: Horton, Mrs. Harper, and Whitman," *Journal of Negro History* 2, No. 4 (October 1917): 386

VERNON LOGGINS   Horton's verse occupies a middle ground between the naturalness of Jupiter Hammon's pieces and such sophisticated imitation as distinguishes the poems of Phillis Wheatley. Echoes of familiar Methodist hymns are heard throughout *Hope of Liberty* and *Naked Genius*. There are also echoes of Pope, Byron, Tom Moore, Burns, and even Milton, all of whom Horton undoubtedly read or heard read. But he did not have Phillis Wheatley's talent for absorbing the music of great poets. He got it all mixed up, and brought in much of his own invention. Therefore, one is likely to hear in his verse a curious mingling of the rhythms of "Come, Thou Fount of Every Blessing," *Paradise Lost,* and the Negro folk song. ⟨. . .⟩

In 1843, an unsuccessful attempt was made to have some of Horton's poems published in the *Southern Literary Messenger.* They are certainly not of a merit to be considered suitable for publication in a magazine of artistic standards. But because they are so pronouncedly inartistic, they are possibly today of greater interest than much of the verse which was printed in the *Southern Literary Messenger.* In Horton's grotesque music and bizarre imagination something which is foreign to the Caucasian mind is delightfully revealed. As veiled as it appears in his conventional hymn-like meters, it is easily recognizable. For the Negro folk song has made it familiar. Moreover, Horton's poems expose the author as a most interesting person. They make us realize that a certain poetic temperament, that manifesting itself in an exuberance which no human force can crush, is as likely to appear in an African slave as in a roving French thief or a tippling Scotch peasant.

> Vernon Loggins, *The Negro Author: His Development in America* (New York: Columbia University Press, 1931), pp. 115–17

RICHARD WALSER   A strange creature with the egotistical pride of having accomplished more in life than ever could have been expected of one so lowly born and so inadequately educated, George Moses Horton was nevertheless a man of courtesy, humility, and good morals. His reputation for honesty, if not always for manual labor, was secure. As a young man, he was described by Caroline Lee Hentz as "unpretending . . . as superior to his tribe as your imagination can picture him. Instead of the broad smile of the African, he has the mild gravity of a Grecian philosopher." And through a long life with its vicissitudes of fortune, these characteristics had been reasonably constant. To them had been added a jovial grandstand manner which he had discovered to be helpful. Most of his white friends loved him for it; for underneath his airy, entertaining exterior, was there not a soul of sentiment?

Horton's role had become that of jester to the court. When the court disappeared, as it had when the rulers were dethroned, he saw that he was only one jester among what must have seemed to him a host of jesters— jesters who were not amused after a performance or two. In fact, Horton discovered for himself that the play was tiresome, the audience falling away.

The truth is that Horton felt no conviviality, no comradeship, when he was with those of his own race. If they did not flatter him, he was bored.

If they did not support his plans, he had no further use for them. In Philadelphia his conduct, which had charmed his admirers in the South, soured on the enlightened free Negroes. Shortly after their cordial reception of him, they opened their eyes to his unctuous hauteur, turned their shoulders, and wrenched away. For them, Poet Horton was overbearing, conceited, and offensive.

Then began the years in Philadelphia during which Horton had no biographer to trace his progress. The jottings are bare, the memoranda scarce, the entries disordered. No patron knocked at his door. No fascinated students wrote about him in their diaries, no devotees sent copy on him to the newspapers, no well-wishers prefaced his poems for publication. Yet, George Moses was not idle, despite the absence of documentation. One who knew him at this time wrote that Horton's most productive period began after his reaching Philadelphia and that it continued till his death.

Richard Walser, *The Black Poet* (New York: Philosophical Library, 1966), pp. 103–4

W. EDWARD FARRISON   One cannot read Horton's writings without being impressed by the fact that he took himself seriously as a poet—that he diligently studied the art of poetry, as is evidenced by his experiments with various verse forms and his endeavors—admittedly not always successful—to appeal to the reader's imagination. He was determined to be a poet in spite of the handicap of slavery, the worst of possible handicaps. He was aware that slavery had kept him from getting the education he longed for and knew he needed. He was often discouraged by the fact that in other ways slavery frustrated his genius and his interest in the life of the mind. He himself took note of all of this in a poem entitled "The Obstructions of Genius," which is the last poem in *Naked Genius*. In the second and third of the seven quatrains of this poem he said,

> Throughout my life I've tried the path,
> Which seemed as leading out of gloom,
> Beneath my feet still kindled wrath,
> Genius seemed leading to a tomb.

> No cultivating hand was found,
> To urge the night improving slave,
> Never by freedom's laurel crowned,
> But pushed through hardship to the grave.

Now that slavery had been abolished, however, he was no longer embittered by his experience as a slave. Rather, with malice toward none and with charity for all, he said in the last stanza of the poem,

> Let us the evil now forget,
> Which darkened the Columbian shore,
> Till sun shall fail to rise and set,
> And slavery's cries are heard no more.

At last freedom for the poet for freedom had become more than a word; it had become a reality.

W. Edward Farrison, "George Moses Horton: Poet for Freedom," *CLA Journal* 14, No. 3 (March 1971): 240–41

M. A. RICHMOND   ⟨Horton⟩ was the first slave poet of the South, the first Southern black man to have his poetry published, not only in one volume, but in three that have been preserved and quite likely in more that have been lost. He was the country's first black professional man of letters who earned most of his living from writing. His was the first clear black outcry in poetic form against slavery.

With the lines

> Alas! and I am born for this,
> To wear this slavish chain?

he first struck the chord that has ever since dominated Afro-American poetry. A pioneer in black protest, he was also a pioneer in black pride. "He himself, Othello like, boasted of the purity of his black blood," says a Southern white scholar.

In some of his verse he invites comparison with the great slave of antiquity, Aesop, but his fables bear the imprint of his life's first setting, the early American frontier, and they are flavored with the frontier idiom, with its humor and folk wisdom. In this, too, he was among the pioneers along a trail that many were to follow.

Such heights as he attained seem the more towering for the burdens and obstacles on his ascent. Nothing came easy. Born a slave on a barren plantation in rural North Carolina and bound by slavery for the first sixty-eight years of his life, the mere mastery of reading was an exercise in human ingenuity and tenacity, for literacy among Southern slaves was first discouraged by custom and then prohibited by law. Poetic compositions began to form in his mind before he knew how to set them down on paper. To find an audience for his verse in these circumstances, to gain access to a knowledge of language and form for the perfection of his work, and finally to secure its publication and sale in a Southern state—each of these successive strides was for a rustic slave a miracle of mind and spirit.

Confronted with such pertinacity, one seeks for a passion that could have motivated it. Horton was possessed by such a passion. It was a passion for poetry—and freedom. Poetry, a lonely pursuit he attained by his own incredible effort. Freedom was something else. In his own way he tried to secure his liberation from slavery by purchase, but ultimately it was purchased with much blood in four years of civil war.

> M. A. Richmond, *Bid the Vassal Soar: Interpretive Essays on the Life and Poetry of Phillis Wheatley and George Moses Horton* (Washington, DC: Howard University Press, 1974), pp. 81–82

JOAN R. SHERMAN   "George Moses Horton, Myself" ⟨in *Naked Genius*⟩ returns to the simple diction and heartfelt tone of regret that gave his early antislavery pieces appealing individuality. This monody of a frustrated poet sums up Horton's life-long conviction that he was born to sing and that his Muse and he were wrongfully imprisoned. The poem discloses that sixty-eight years of bondage could not dim Horton's spirit and aspiration:

> I feel myself in need
>   Of the inspiring strains of ancient lore,
> My heart to lift, my empty mind to feed,
>   And all the world explore.
>
> I know that I am old
>   And never can recover what is past,
> But for the future may some light unfold
>   And soar from ages blast.
>
> I feel resolved to try,
>   My wish to prove, my calling to pursue,
> Or mount up from the earth into the sky,
>   To show what Heaven can do.
>
> My genius from a boy,
>   Has fluttered like a bird within my heart;
> But I could not thus confined her powers employ,
>   Impatient to depart.
>
> She like a restless bird,
>   Would spread her wing, her power to be unfurl'd,
> And let her songs be loudly heard,
>   And dart from world to world.

In 1883, Collier Cobb visited the eighty-six-year-old Horton in Philadelphia. "I called him 'Poet' which pleased him greatly," Cobb recalled, "and he told me that I was using his proper title." So it was, because all his life "Poet" was synonymous with "George Moses Horton." He struggled for literacy to write poetry; he begged for manumission to write poetry; he earned modest freedom of movement and a livelihood by writing poetry and continued to write despite the failure of his three volumes and the certainty that untold numbers of poems in manuscript would never be published. Historically, the "Colored Bard of North-Carolina" is a major nineteenth-century poet, the only one to publish volumes of poetry while in bondage, and the first black man to publish any book in the South. From the first, Horton showed a natural talent for capturing the rhythms of verse, a perfect ear for rhyme, and a sensitive, often cynical awareness of what life, and thus poetry, was all about. His *Hope of Liberty* and occasional later folk verses are admirable, and in the context of his life they are superb. Overall, his greatest triumph was to be always Poet Horton.

> Joan R. Sherman, "George Moses Horton," *Invisible Poets: Afro-Americans of the Nineteenth Century* (Urbana: University of Illinois Press, 1974), pp. 18–19

JOHN L. COBBS   To appreciate *Hope of Liberty* we must first understand the context within which it appeared. The Colonies and the early Republic were hardly a congenial climate for the production of great poetry. The works of Bradstreet, Freneau, Taylor, and Bryant are competent and occasionally moving, but only the most chauvinist of readers will call their poetry great. The literary cradles of New England, New York, and Philadelphia rocked out little of real worth in the first two hundred years of American history, and what seems most lasting is philosophical and historical prose. At the time George Moses Horton and his sponsors brought out *Hope of Liberty*, only one truly major American poet had published, Poe with his slender and unacclaimed *Tamerlane* in 1827. The accomplishments of Emerson, Longfellow, Whitman, and Dickinson lay in the future.

Furthermore, poetry, even more than prose, through the first quarter of the nineteenth century, had been the product of the Northeast. The agrarian South was poor enough soil for intellectual development of any kind, but it was particularly hostile to the rarified flights of poetic fancy. Significantly, the first two black poets to publish in America, Jupiter Hammon and Phillis Wheatley, came respectively from New York and New England.

George Moses Horton, however, came from the rural part of a slave state. True, he was exposed from his late teens to the limited intellectual stimulation of the University of North Carolina at Chapel Hill, but we know from the memoirs of one of his mentors, Caroline Lee Hentz, that Chapel Hill in the 1820s could be pretty stultifying, even for the wife of a faculty member. How much more so for a slave who could only get to town on occasional trips, who worked the fields of his master James Horton in another county. It was remarkable, then, that *Hope of Liberty* appeared in 1829, when Horton was about thirty-two, the first book by a black poet in America in fifty years. ⟨. . .⟩

Hope of Liberty is a more appropriately titled volume than is at first evident. Far from being a random collection of verses on a variety of uncon-nected subjects, it is informed by a thematic integrity. Each poem shows an ongoing poetic concern with the projection of this single image. George Moses Horton's "hope of liberty" was a hope of the liberty to flee and the liberty to fly. This twofold sense of the meaning of flight is expressed throughout the poems of this pioneer volume by an American black poet, and the consistency of that expression gives *Hope of Liberty* a unity that makes it a worthy and distinguished work to stand at the gateways of American black poetry.

> John L. Cobbs, "George Moses Horton's *Hope of Liberty*: Thematic Unity in Early American Black Poetry," *CLA Journal* 24, No. 4 (June 1981): 441–42, 450

BLYDEN JACKSON   He was, as a person, uncommon. What would have happened to him had he been born a field hand on one of the huge, comparatively impersonal plantations operative upon the rice lands of South Carolina or distributed here and there throughout the cotton kingdoms of the Deep South defies, of course, ordinary conjecture. The power, almost incredibly strong in him, that would not let him rest until he created poetry may have withstood the pressures which the dehumanizing environment and the crippling rigors of an existence so cruel and physically exhausting would have imposed upon it. But such an even greater miracle than the miracle he actually was did not, and thus now will not, occur. No poet more enslaved, *de jure* and de facto, than Horton ever has written, or ever will write, poetry in America. And yet Horton did write poetry, in the often paranoid slaveholder's South. He wrote there, moreover, the poetry, whatever its merit or demerit, of a true poet, of one for whom, indeed, the writing of poetry, whatever its nature or subject, was an inescapable accompaniment to the very act of breathing. There has been argument as to how racial a poet Horton was. There can be no argument as to how compulsive were his years of cultivating his muse. He was, in his own small way, a Villon, a Poe, a Rimbaud, an Ezra Pound, a fated and doomed follower of an art for that art's sake. He did not need, then, to write against racism. The kind of person, and artist, he was did that for him. For all of his life he was black. Yet, also, for most of his life he was an object lesson in the irrelevance of color to aesthetic sensibility. He was, in other words, a living refutation of racism's major premise, that Negroes are born unlike other people because they are born less human.

> Blyden Jackson, *A History of Afro-American Literature* (Baton Rouge: Louisiana State University Press, 1989), Vol. 1, p. 84

◈ *Bibliography*

The Hope of Liberty: Containing a Number of Poetical Pieces. 1829, 1837 (as *Poems by a Slave*).

Poetical Works. 1845.

[*Oration, Delivered before the Fraternity of Pedlars, at Auburn.* 1847.]

Naked Genius. Ed. Will H. S. Banks. 1865.

※ ※ ※

James Weldon Johnson
1871–1938

NEITHER OF JAMES WELDON JOHNSON'S parents had been slaves before the
Civil War. His father, James, was born free in Virginia in 1830; his mother,
Helen Duttel, was part Haitian, part French, and a member of the Bahamian
black middle class. James William ("James Weldon" after 1913) was born
on June 17, 1871, in Jacksonville, Florida, after his family escaped the
economic depression in Nassau at that time.

In Florida, James, Sr., provided his family with a middle-class life accessible
to only a small minority of blacks in the South of the late 1800s. As a
teenager, Johnson visited New York and became fascinated with city life.
At seventeen he worked as a secretary to a white physician and research
scientist, Thomas Osmond Summers, whose character greatly influenced
him. Summers saw Johnson as a social equal, encouraging the young man
to read and write poetry.

At Atlanta University, modeled after Yale, Johnson received a classical
education and wished to pursue public service; he was often an active
participant in formal debates on the issue of race. Upon graduation, and
after a stint as a principal, Johnson established the first high school for
blacks, as well as creating America's first black daily newspaper, the Jacksonville *Daily American.* Upon its financial collapse, Johnson studied law and
in 1896 was admitted to the Florida bar.

Johnson practiced law for part of the year but traveled to New York in
the summer months to work with his brother, John Rosamond, and other
black performers bound for Broadway and Europe. The Johnson brothers
employed popular black imagery but avoided standard racist vocabulary.
One of the earliest songs composed by the Johnsons, "Lift Every Voice and
Sing," was composed for a celebration of Abraham Lincoln's birthday in
1900; this song was later adopted by the NAACP as their official song.

Johnson, in his early dialect poems and lyrics, drew upon a genre full of
racial stereotypes, but he also accepted the reality of that dialect as an
authentic language. He wished to reveal the deeper themes of history and

the emotions of black Americans; yet he, and his critics as well, found the use of dialect problematic at best. Even today it continues to be a topic for debate.

In 1906 Johnson entered foreign service as a U.S. consul in Venezuela and wrote his only work of fiction, *The Autobiography of an Ex-Colored Man* (published anonymously in 1912), a story modeled on an autobiographical narrative. After publishing his first book of poems, *Fifty Years and Other Poems* (1917), Johnson became Secretary of the NAACP and led a battle for a federal antilynching law, using his talents as a lawyer, public speaker, and lobbyist. Johnson was perhaps the leading proponent of black American culture in the 1920s. However, he became increasingly at odds with other black leaders and rejected communism, separatism, and violence as alternatives in the struggle for racial equality.

In 1930 Johnson published *Black Manhattan,* a still valuable study of black theatre in New York. His autobiography, *Along This Way,* followed in 1933. The last books to appear in his lifetime were the trenchant essay *Negro Americans, What Now?* (1934) and a selection of his poetry, *Saint Peter Relates an Incident* (1935).

Johnson died a sudden death when, on his sixty-seventh birthday (June 17, 1938), his automobile collided with a train while he was vacationing in Maine. He is buried in Greenwood Cemetery in Brooklyn, New York.

◈ *Critical Extracts*

BRANDER MATTHEWS   In the following pages Mr. James Weldon Johnson ⟨. . .⟩ gathers together a group of lyrics, delicate in workmanship, fragrant with sentiment, and phrased in pure and unexceptionable English. Then he has another group of dialect verses, racy of the soil, pungent in flavor, swinging in rhythm and adroit in rhyme. But where he shows himself as a pioneer is the half-dozen larger and bolder poems, of a loftier strain, in which he has been nobly successful in expressing the higher aspirations of his own people. It is in uttering this cry for recognition, for sympathy, for understanding, and above all, for justice, that Mr. Johnson is most original and most powerful. In the superb and soaring stanzas of "Fifty Years" (published exactly half-a-century after the signing of the Emancipation Proclamation) he has given us one of the noblest commemorative poems yet written by any American,—a poem sonorous in its diction, vigorous in its workmanship, elevated in its imagination and sincere in its emotion. In it speaks the voice of his race; and the race is fortunate in its spokesman. In it a fine theme has been finely treated. In it we are made to see something of the soul of the people who are our fellow citizens now and forever,— even if we do not always so regard them. In it we are glad to acclaim a poem which any living poet might be proud to call his own.

> Brander Matthews, "Preface," *Fifty Years and Other Poems* by James Weldon Johnson (Boston: Cornhill Co., 1917), pp. xiii–xiv

ROBERT T. KERLIN   Now of New York, but born in Florida and reared in the South, James Weldon Johnson is a man of various abilities, acomplishments, and activities. He was graduated with the degrees of A.B. and A.M. from Atlanta University and later studied for three years in Columbia University. First a school-principal, then a practitioner of the law, he followed at last the strongest propensity and turned author. His literary work includes eight light operas, for which his brother, J. Rosamond Johnson, composed the music, and a novel entitled *The Autobiography of an Ex-Colored Man*. Having been United States consul in two Latin-American countries, he is a master of Spanish and has made translations of Spanish plays and poems. The English libretto of *Goyescas* was made by him for the Metropolitan Opera Company in 1915. He is also one of the ablest editorial writers in the country. In the *Public Ledger*'s contest of 1916 he won the third prize. His editorials are widely syndicated in the Negro weekly press. Poems of his have appeared in *The Century, The Crisis,* and *The Independent.*

Professor Brander Matthews in his introduction to *Fifty Years and Other Poems* speaks of the "superb and soaring stanzas" of the title-poem and describes it as "a poem sonorous in its diction, vigorous in its workmanship, elevated in its imagination, and sincere in its emotion." Doubtless this will seem like the language of exaggeration. The sceptic, however, must withhold judgement until he has read the poem ⟨. . .⟩

> Robert T. Kerlin, *Negro Poets and Their Poems* (Washington, DC: Associated Publishers, 1923), pp. 90–91

JAMES WELDON JOHNSON   In a general way, these poems were suggested by the rather vague memories of sermons I heard preached in my childhood; but the immediate stimulus for setting them down came quite definitely at a comparatively recent date. I was speaking on a Sunday in Kansas City, addressing meetings in various colored churches. When I had finished my fourth talk it was after nine o'clock at night, but the committee told me there was still another meeting to address. I demurred, making the quotation about the willingness of the spirit and the weakness of the flesh, for I was dead tired. I also protested the lateness of the hour, but I was informed that for the meeting at this church we were in good time. When we reached the church an "exhorter" was just concluding a dull sermon. After his there were two short sermons. These sermons proved to be preliminaries, mere curtain-raisers for a famed visiting preacher. At last he arose. He was a dark-brown man, handsome in his gigantic proportions. He appeared to be a bit self-conscious, perhaps impressed by the presence of the "distinguished visitor" on the platform, and started in to preach a formal sermon from a formal text. The congregation sat apathetic and dozing. He sensed that he was losing his audience and his opportunity. Suddenly he closed the Bible, stepped out from behind the pulpit and began to preach. He started intoning the old folk-sermon that begins with the creation of the world and ends with Judgement Day. He was at once a changed man, free, at ease and masterful. The change in the congregation was instantaneous. An electric current ran through the crowd. It was in a moment alive and quivering; and all the while the preacher held it in the palm of his hand. He was wonderful in the way he employed his conscious and unconscious art. He strode the pulpit up and down in what was actually a very rhythmic dance, and he brought into play the full gamut of his wonderful voice, a voice—what shall I say?—not of an organ or a trumpet, but rather of a trombone, the instrument possessing above all the others the power to express the wide and varied range of emotions encompassed by the human voice—and with greater amplitude. He intoned, he moaned, he pleaded— he blared, he crashed, he thundered. I sat fascinated; and more, I was, perhaps against my will, deeply moved; the emotional effect upon me was irresistible. Before he had finished I took a slip of paper and somewhat surreptitiously jotted down some ideas for the first poem, "The Creation."

James Weldon Johnson, "Preface," *God's Trombones* (New York: Viking Press, 1927), pp. 5–7

COUNTEE CULLEN   James Weldon Johnson has blown the true spirit of the pentecostal trumpeting of the dark Joshuas of the race in *God's Trombones*, composed of seven sermon-poems and a prayer. The seven sermons are like the seven blasts blown by Joshua at Jericho. "The Creation", "The Prodigal Son", "Go Down Death—A Funeral Sermon", "Noah Built the Ark", "The Crucifixion", "Let My People Go", and "The Judgement Day", they are all great evangelical texts. And the magnificent manner in which they are done increases our regret that Mr. Johnson was not intrigued into preaching "The Dry Bones in the Valley", the *pièce de résistance* in the repertoire of every revivalist to whom a good shout is a recommendation of salvation well received. ⟨. . .⟩

The poet here has admirably risen to his intentions and his needs; entombed in this bright mausoleum the Negro preacher of an older day can never pass entirely deathward. Dialect could never have been synthesized into the rich mortar necessary for these sturdy unrhymed exhortations. Mr. Johnson has captured the peculiar flavor of speech by which the black sons of Zebedee, lacking academic education, but grounded through their religious intensity in the purest marshalling of the English language (the King James' version of the Bible) must have astounded men more obviously letter-trained. This verse is simple and awful at once, the grand diapason of a musician playing on an organ with far more than two keys.

There is a universality of appeal and appreciation in these poems that raises them, despite the fact that they are labled "Seven Negro Sermons in Verse", and despite the persistent racial emphasis of Mr. Douglas' beautiful illustrations, far above a relegation to any particular group of people. Long ago the recital of the agonies and persecutions of the Hebrew children under Pharaoh ceased to chronicle the tribulations of one people alone. So in "Let My People Go" there is a world-wide cry from the oppressed against the oppressor, from the frail and puny against the arrogant in strength who hold them against their will. From Beersheba to Dan the trusting wrench, rich in nothing but his hope and faith, holds this axiomatic solace:

> Listen!—Listen!
> All you sons of Pharaoh,
> Who do you think can hold God's people
> When the Lord himself has said,
> Let my people go?

Countee Cullen, "And the Walls Came Tumblin' Down," *Bookman* (New York) 66, No. 2 (October 1927): 221

HARRIET MONROE   For some time Mr. Johnson has been known as a leader among the American Negro poets, and as by all odds their best editor. His *Book of American Negro Poetry*, and his two books of *Spirituals*, with their prefaces, are monuments of patient and sympathetic scholarship and of devotion to his race in its highest achievements.

The present volume is his own highest achievement as a poet. The author says modestly in his excellent preface:

> I claim no more for these poems than that I have written them after the manner of the primitive sermons.

But it is something of an achievement to suggest, as he does, the spirit and rhythm of those sermons, and to do it without the help of dialect or of antiphonal repetitions. There may be two opinions about the tradition of dialect; at least Mr. Johnson makes a very good argument against it in his preface, and gets on very well without it. ⟨. . .⟩

We have space for only a hint of the book's quality. Mr. Johnson does not claim to have originated the sermons; like Joel Chandler Harris he has set down what he heard—the essence of it; and he is entitled to credit of the same kind. Hardly to the same degree, however, as the authenticity is less complete, the art less perfect. I wish he could have let himself go a little more rashly; for the creation of myth, as I heard Lucine Finch repeat her old mammy's version, was more powerfully poetic than Mr. Johnson's.

Harriet Monroe, "Negro Sermons," *Poetry* 30, No. 5 (August 1927): 291–93

CARL VAN DOREN   With an energy beyond what was needed for his writing, he busied himself with Republican politics. Having gradually outgrown Jacksonville, he now gradually outgrew Broadway. In 1905 he was appointed by Theodore Roosevelt to the post of United States Consul at Puerto Cabello, Venezuela.

Already proficient in Spanish and acquainted with the simpler forms of politics, he enjoyed what was virtually a sinecure in Venezuela, and later in Corinto, Nicaragua, ably represented his government through a difficult period of revolutionary confusion, without ceasing to write. After the election of Woodrow Wilson both race prejudice and politics stood, Mr. Johnson saw, between him and promotion. He left the consular service and returned to New York, where for ten years he wrote the editorials in a Negro newspaper. In 1916 he became Field Secretary of the newly formed National Association for the Advancement of Colored People. ⟨. . .⟩

The United States has not deserved James Weldon Johnson. Fitted to be a statesman of high rank anywhere, he has been confined by race prejudice to action within a minority. There can be no question that this has limited him. His life deals with black America, or with black America in its relations to white, not with all America during the past half century. A white man of affairs with half Mr. Johnson's gifts might have come into contact with twice as many people of first-rate importance. What it must have cost James Weldon Johnson to realize this, as he must have realized it, he does not say or hint. He seems early to have accepted the unmistakable bounds within which he would have to work, to have made the best of them, and to have saved for clear-sighted action the force which another Negro might have spent in blind rebellion. To be teacher, lawyer, poet, consul, journalist was never enough for him.

Something had to be done about the plight of his race in America, and he has done as much as any man alive.

Carl Van Doren, "A Citizen of Whom America Can Be Proud," *New York Herald Tribune Books*, 1 October 1933, pp. 1, 7

DAVID LITTLEJOHN   James Weldon Johnson, a contemporary of Dunbar's, outlived him to become one of the most distinguished Negro Americans of his time; a lyricist for Broadway shows, U.S. Consul in Venezuela and Nicaragua, a teacher, attorney, novelist, poet, editor, professor, and executive secretary of the NAACP. His autobiography, *Along This Way*, is one of the more dependable and readable of Negro leaders' autobiographies. His noteworthy "serious" poems are black propaganda pieces in nineteenth-century rhetoric, on the "This Land is Our Land" theme; they include, in "Brothers" (1917), what may be the first outspoken dramatization of a lynching in verse.

His claim to a degree of poetic celebrity, however, rests on *God's Trombones* and "St. Peter Relates an Incident," both written well after the end of the period in question, though still obviously the work of an older writer. The former, a collection of seven imitations of Negro sermons, once appeared striking and original; but so many examples of the colored preacher's sermon have appeared since (Faulkner's, Ellison's, Baldwin's, Ossie Davis', etc.), examples more compulsive, more striking and effective, that Johnson's versions may read today like tame, overcivilized outlines, without the real spirit, the crescendo rhythms, the extraordinary imagery one associates with the genre. Although "The Creation" is the best known, "Judgement Day" strikes me as the best, the most rhapsodic and rolling. Certain sequences of the others are effective ⟨. . .⟩ But the collection as a whole still seems slightly anthropological-condescending, a book of imitations far less potent than their originals.

David Littlejohn, *Black on White: A Critical Survey of Writing by American Negroes* (New York: Grossman Publishers, 1966), pp. 24–25

RICHARD A. LONG   The verse output of James Weldon Johnson falls into four groups: lyrics in standard English, poems in the dialect tradition, folk-inspired free verse, and a long satirical poem. The first two groups are contemporary and were published in the volume *Fifty Years and Other Poems* (Boston, 1917). The prayer and seven Negro sermons of the third group constitute *God's Trombones* (New York, 1927). The last group is represented by the poem "St. Peter Relates an Incident of the Resurrection Day," privately printed in 1930, and republished with a selection of earlier poems in 1935.

The early poetry of Johnson belongs to the late nineteenth century tradition of sentimental poetry in so far as its techniques and verse forms are concerned, seldom rising above the mediocrity characteristic of American poetry in the period 1890–1910, during which it was written for the most part. In purpose, however, Johnson's early verse was a species of propaganda, designed sometimes overtly, sometimes obliquely, to advance to a reading public the merits and the grievances of blacks. In this sense the poetry of Johnson is an integral part of a coherent strain in the poetry of Afro-Americans beginning with Phillis Wheatley:

> Remember, Christians, Negroes, black as Cain,
> May be refined, and join th' angelic train.
>   (Phillis Wheatley, "On Being Brought from Africa
>   to America")

More particularly we may note the relationship of Johnson's early poetry to that of Paul Laurence Dunbar, his much admired friend and contemporary. Though they were about the same age, Dunbar was by far the more precocious, and his virtuosity had an obvious impact on Johnson, though little of Dunbar's verse bears any obvious burden of racial protest, in spite of the real personal suffering Dunbar underwent because of misunderstanding and neglect that he ascribed to his color.

Another factor of importance in the early verse of Johnson is his composition of verses to be set to music by his brother J. Rosamond Johnson; the search for euphony and piquancy and the use of devices such as internal rhyme betrays the hand of the librettist.

The division of Johnson's poetry into standard lyrics and dialect verse, as in the case of Dunbar's poetry, reflects a self-conscious distinction made by the author himself. Johnson's first collection of his poetry, which appeared eleven years after Dunbar's death, presents forty-eight standard poems, followed by a segregated group of sixteen "Jingles and Croons." The dialect poems reflect of course a literary tradition of their own since in point of fact the themes and forms of such a dialect of poetry as was written by Dunbar and Johnson and many others reflects no tradition of the folk who used "dialect." In point of fact, it is useful to remember that the dialect poets learned mainly from their predecessors and employ for the most part uniform grammatical and orthographic conventions which suggest that they did not consciously seek to represent any individual or regional dialect. Johnson himself gives a brief account of the dialect literary tradition in his introductions to Dunbar and other dialect poets in *The Book of American Negro Poetry* (New York, 1931).

Richard A. Long, "A Weapon of My Song: The Poetry of James Weldon Johnson," *Phylon* 32, No. 4 (Winter 1971): 374–75

EUGENE LEVY   Like many creative writers, Johnson felt that art and social criticism were fundamentally different forms of expression, though each might be of use to the other. Art could not be produced for the purpose of propaganda. Art such as Forster's *A Passage to India* or the singing of Ethel Waters, however, in certain subtle ways could expand our understanding of a social problem like racism. Writers such as McKay and Hughes, Johnson believed, demonstrated to the American public that black men could create valid art by drawing for their material upon a significant social phenomenon—the life of the Afro-American. Johnson saw this as contributing to the breakdown of racial separation in American society, thus pushing society closer to his goal of integration.

For those who believed that goal to be both invalid and unrealizable, however, men like Hughes, McKay, and Johnson were simply deceiving blacks when they claimed that demonstrating one's ability would bring opportunity. Perhaps the most outspoken advocate in the 1920s of this viewpoint was Marcus Garvey, a man with few friends among intellectuals, either black or white. Garvey did nothing to conceal the profound distrust he felt toward whites, or toward blacks who tried to convince whites they ought to share the wealth and power of Euro-America with its black population. W. E. B. Du Bois, one of Garvey's most vitriolic critics, nevertheless shared with the Back to Africa leader a profound skepticism toward putting faith in whites. The white power structure, at least as it existed in the United States in the 1920s, seemed unlikely to be converted to brotherhood by the artistry of Ethel Waters or the insight of Gertrude Stein. Along with the sexual prudery of his views toward the Renaissance, Du Bois firmly believed that only the fist of hard-hitting propaganda, not the velvet glove of art, would stop the oppression of white over black.

On one matter Garvey, Du Bois, Johnson, and the writers of the Renaissance agreed: the necessity of pride in the race's past and present accomplishments. Booker T. Washington expressed it for them when he wrote: "It was with a race as it is with an individual: it must respect itself if it would win the respect of others." Johnson, along with most of the younger writers, however, was far more optimistic than Garvey or Du Bois as to the influence black writers might have on American society. He had his differences with the younger writers, largely stemming from his attachment to what was essentially a modified "melting pot" conception of America's future. Blacks should further develop their own culture so as to establish themselves in American society, but, once that had been accomplished, it would be wisest and safest, Johnson had maintained for many years, to meld into a fully unified national culture. Black writers such as Locke, Hughes, and Countee Cullen, on the other hand, put much more emphasis on maintaining a unique black culture. They adhered to a "nation of nations" conception: black Americans, like Euro-American ethnic groups, would develop their own hyphenated culture, but all Americans would cooperate in maintaining an equitable and productive society. Such differences in ends were theoretical in the social situation of the 1920s. Those of the Renaissance agreed on means, and especially on the role of art in race progress and reconciliation. After reading *The Autobiography of an Ex-Colored Man*, Aaron Douglas— the black artist who illustrated many of the books of the Renaissance, including *God's Trombones*—wrote Johnson: "The post-war Negro, blinded by the glare and almost sudden bursting of a new day, finds much difficulty in realizing the immense power and effort . . . the pre-war Negro . . . made to prepare the country for what we now feel to be the new awakening." The "new awakening," of course, awoke fewer than Douglas, in his enthusiasm, seemed to think—a fact many black writers were to learn in the 1930s. Nevertheless, the sense of change as well as of continuity with the past which he expressed in his letter reflected both a feeling and a reality which Johnson had done much to foster.

Eugene Levy, *James Weldon Johnson: Black Leader, Black Voice* (Chicago: University of Chicago Press, 1973), pp. 219–21

ARTHUR P. DAVIS   The second volume, *God's Trombones*, though appearing only ten years after the first, shows far more than ten years of poetic growth and understanding on the part of Johnson. An index to this maturing is found in the preface to *The Book of American Negro Poetry*, an anthology published in 1922. In this lengthy preface Johnson voiced his dissatisfaction with the limitations of dialect writing and his interest in a new vehicle for Negro expression:

> What the colored poet in the United States needs to do is
> something like what Synge did for the Irish; he needs to find a
> form that will express the racial spirit by symbols from within
> rather than by symbols from without, such as the mere mutilation
> of English spelling and pronunciation. He needs a form that is
> freer and larger than dialect, but which will still hold the racial
> flavor; a form of expressing imagery, the idioms, the peculiar turns
> of thought, and the distinctive humor and pathos, too, of the
> Negro, but which will also be capable of voicing the deepest and
> highest emotions and aspirations, and allow the widest range of
> subject and the widest scope of treatment.

In *God's Trombones*, using the old-time Negro folk sermon as his vehicle, Johnson successfully puts his theories into practice. In these eight free-verse poems, without the distortion and limitation of dialect, he captures the rhythm, intonation (as far as one can write it down), sentence structure, breaks, and repetitions of the illiterate black folk preacher. Johnson has shown great skill in transforming folk material into sophisticated art. Note, for example, how he renders the characteristic intoning of the folk sermon; note the interrupted flow of the phrases, the dramatic breaks:

> Jesus, my sorrowing Jesus,
> The sweat like drops of blood upon his brow,
> Talking with his Father,
> While the three disciples slept,
> Saying: Father,
> Oh, Father,
> Not as I will
> Not as I will,
> But let thy will be done.

The spiritual as well as the sermon influence is found in these free-verse poems. Johnson's success with these folk forms had considerable effect on the later Renaissance writers. It gave impetus to the folk emphasis which characterized much Renaissance verse. Johnson used the spiritual sermon and, of course, certain forms common to dialectic poetry. Langston Hughes,

Sterling Brown, Waring Cuney, and others added ballad and blues forms and otherwise widened the range of folk expression. Johnson, however, was a pioneer influence. He saw the possibilities of folk influence as early as 1922. Because of its folk undergirding, *God's Trombones*, in all probability, will outlast the rest of Johnson's poetry.

> Arthur P. Davis, *From the Dark Tower: Afro-American Writers 1900 to 1960* (Washington, DC: Howard University Press, 1974), pp. 28–29

LADELL PAYNE   It is as a writer that Johnson is best remembered. And like other black writers from the South, Johnson is a recognizable part of a Southern literary movement that includes both blacks and whites. As had Charles Waddell Chesnutt, ⟨. . .⟩ James Weldon Johnson drew upon both Negro folklore and his own experiences as a Southern black for the subject matter of his writing. Chesnutt presented Negro folk tales in his conjure stories; Johnson collected spirituals and in *God's Trombones* preserved the cadences of the Negro folk sermon. But Johnson was a more restrained, conscious artist than was Chesnutt. Like Joel Chandler Harris, Chesnutt used dialect extensively in his conjure stories and, when depicting the speech of uneducated blacks, in his novels; Johnson avoided dialect because he felt it was looked upon almost exclusively as a source either of pathos or of humor and these were not the effects he was after. Yet in works such as *God's Trombones*, Johnson clearly suggests Southern Negro church speech through his reproduction of the Southern black minister's characteristic rhetorical devices—the repetitions, the alliterations, the pauses, the echoes from the King James Bible, the folk images—all of which show that he was as conscious of dialectical nuances as was Twain in writing *Adventures of Huckleberry Finn* or Faulkner in writing the Rev'un Shegog's Easter sermon in *The Sound and the Fury*. Johnson's ability to create the effect of dialect without using its typical spellings or illiteracies is one of his greatest skills as an artist.

> Ladell Payne, "Themes and Cadences: James Weldon Johnson's Novel," *Southern Literary Journal* 11, No. 2 (Spring 1979): 44–45

CHIDI IKONNÉ   In a way, *The Autobiography of an Ex-Colored Man* is a celebration of the Negro folk. This can also be said of James Weldon Johnson's more serious dialect poems—such as the lilting lullaby entitled

"De Little Pickaninny's Gone to Sleep," and the folktale "Brer Rabbit, You's de Cutes' of 'em All" which dramatizes the mythical weakness of the overconfident and aggressively strong in the face of the bodily weak but mentally strong nature. It is, however, in "The Creation" (1918) that the exaltation reached its apogee in Johnson's work, at least before this Negro sermon was combined with other poems like it and published in the volumes of *God's Trombones* (1927).

Operating from the consciousness of a folk preacher, who speaks to a group of believers whose lives, like his, are rooted in warm human relations, in the soil, the water, and other elements of nature (from which they derive all their needs including "pictures," to use Zora Neale Hurston's terms, with which to "adorn" their "expression") the poem is simple and direct. It eschews metaphysical abstractions and reflects the conception of *Obatala*, God the creator, in the Negro folklore: a being more human than the Bible concedes. Thus he feels lonely and seeks company. He almost suffers from the blues. He smiles in happiness. Zora Neale Hurston, the folklorist, as distinct from the fictionist, documents this concept of a human God:

> Negro folklore is not a thing of the past. . . . God and the Devil are paired, and are treated no more reverently than Rockefeller and Ford. . . . The angels and the apostles walk and talk like section hands. And through it all walks Jack, the greatest culture hero of the South; Jack beats them all—even the Devil, who is often smarter than God.
>
> The Devil is next after Jack as a culture hero. He can outsmart everyone but Jack. God is absolutely no match for him. He is good-natured and full of humour.

Chidi Ikonné, *From Du Bois to Van Vechten: The Early New Negro Literature 1903–1926* (Westport, CT: Greenwood Press, 1981), pp. 70–71

SUSAN J. KOPRINCE   A study of the women in Johnson's sermons ⟨. . .⟩ not only reveals the poet's attitude toward the female sex, but, in a broader sense, helps to explain his enchantment with Harlem during the 1920s—the same Harlem which Johnson evokes so vividly in his cultural treatise *Black Manhattan* (1930).

Several poetic sermons in *God's Trombones* make clear Johnson's view of women as powerful temptresses. The poem "Noah Built the Ark" introduces the figure of Eve, the archetypal temptress "With nothing to do the whole day long / But play all around in the garden" with her consort, Adam. Although Eve disobeys God out of vanity ("You're surely goodlooking," Satan tells her, offering her a mirror), Adam does so out of uxoriousness and a fatal desire for this beautiful, sensuous woman. "Back there, six thousand years ago," Johnson says, "Man first fell by woman— / Lord, and he's doing the same today." ⟨. . .⟩

But Johnson also presents a different image of women in *God's Trombones*: that of the saintly mother, the sympathetic and loving comforter. In his sermon "The Crucifixion," for instance, Johnson pictures the Virgin Mary at the scene of her son's death, weeping as she watches "her sweet, baby Jesus on the cruel cross." ⟨. . .⟩

So important for Johnson is this dichotomy between the sensual and the spiritual, between the whorish and the maternal, that he employs it not only to describe the women of *God's Trombones*, but to depict Harlem of the twenties in his cultural study *Black Manhattan*. Just as Johnson tends to divide women into two extreme types—the sexual temptress and the saintly mother—so does he picture Harlem as a city containing the extremes of sensuality and spirituality. For Johnson, Harlem is at once a voluptuous temptress and a spiritual mother—a force which inspires both amorous passion and creative genius—a city which is seductive and vibrant.

> Susan J. Koprince, "Femininity and the Harlem Experience: A Note on James Weldon Johnson," *CLA Journal* 29, No. 1 (September 1985): 52–54

▦ *Bibliography*

The Autobiography of an Ex-Colored Man. 1912.

Fifty Years and Other Poems. 1917.

The Changing Status of Negro Labor. 1918.

Africa in the World Democracy (with others). 1919.

Self-Determining Haiti. 1920.

The Book of American Negro Poetry (editor). 1922, 1931.

The Race Problem and Peace. c. 1924.

The Book of Negro Spirituals (editor; with J. Rosamond Johnson). 1925.

The Second Book of American Negro Spirituals (editor; with J. Rosamond Johnson). 1926.

God's Trombones: Seven Negro Sermons in Verse. 1927.

Native African Races and Culture. 1927.

Saint Peter Relates an Incident of the Resurrection Day. 1930.

Black Manhattan. 1930.
The Shining Life: An Appreciation of Julius Rosenwald. 1932.
Along This Way: The Autobiography of James Weldon Johnson. 1933.
Negro Americans, What Now? 1934.
Saint Peter Relates an Incident: Selected Poems. 1935.

Oscar Micheaux
1884–1951

OSCAR MICHEAUX was born on January 2, 1884, on a farm near Metropolis, Illinois, the fifth of thirteen children of Calvin and Belle Willingham Michaux (the original spelling of the name). Although educated in schools in Metropolis, Micheaux was not satisfied with the insular life there and left at the age of seventeen. After holding a series of menial jobs, including porter on a Pullman car, he headed west, occupying a small homestead in Gregory County, South Dakota. It was this experience that led him to write his first work, *The Conquest: The Story of a Negro Pioneer* (1913), published anonymously as "By the Pioneer." This work is frequently assumed to be a novel, but—in spite of the fact that the protagonist's name is altered to Oscar Devereaux and other names are changed—it is in fact Micheaux's autobiography. The work is dedicated to Booker T. Washington, whose belief in the uplifting of the black race through hard work and self-discipline Micheaux had adopted.

Micheaux became his own salesman for *The Conquest,* traveling throughout South Dakota and then the South to sell copies of it. This enterprise proved so successful that Micheaux founded his own publishing company, the Western Book Supply, then based in Lincoln, Nebraska, and in 1915 issued his first true novel, *The Forged Note: A Romance of the Darker Races.* This work is also very autobiographical: it features a protagonist who is a homesteader in South Dakota and the author of a book of his experiences, and who then undertakes to sell copies of his book through the South. This framework allows Micheaux to focus on the problems of blacks in the South, problems Micheaux evidently believed to be largely self-caused because of a lack of moral strength on the part of blacks and the lack of a cohesive social structure that would allow blacks to assist each other.

Micheaux's next novel, *The Homesteader* (1917), also published by the Western Book Supply (now in Sioux City, Iowa), is a romance involving a love triangle between a black man, a white woman, and a black woman. The book, although melodramatic and with a contrived happy ending, interested the Lincoln Motion Picture Company, a firm devoted to producing films by blacks for black audiences. Micheaux could not come to terms with the company and boldly decided to film the book himself, although he had no experience in film. The film, appearing in 1922, was a relative success and permitted Micheaux to form the Micheaux Book and Film Company.

For the next twenty years Micheaux abandoned writing and devoted himself to writing, producing, and directing films, although many of these are lost. He produced many silent films in the 1920s, including *Body and Soul* (1925), in which Paul Robeson made his screen debut, and adaptations of two works by Charles W. Chesnutt, *The Conjure Woman* (1926) and *The House Behind the Cedars* (1927). Micheaux's company went into bankruptcy in 1928 but was saved by the contributions of white financiers. In 1931 Micheaux produced the first all-black talkie, *The Exile*. Throughout his film career Micheaux faced criticism for the low production quality of his films and for the frequently negative depictions of blacks in them.

In the 1940s Micheaux decided to resume writing, but his later works were not successful. *The Wind from Nowhere* (1941) is a reworking of *The Conquest*; *The Case of Mrs. Wingate* (1944) is a thriller involving Nazi spies and a black detective; *The Story of Dorothy Stanfield* (1946) is a sensational novel about an insurance scam; and *The Masquerade* (1947) is a transparent reworking of Chesnutt's *The House Behind the Cedars*. His last film was *Betrayal* (1948). Oscar Micheaux died on a book tour in Charlotte, North Carolina, on March 26, 1951.

◈ *Critical Extracts*

HOWARD A. PHELPS   The most popular author of the city is Oscar Micheaux, the author of *The Homesteader*. He supervised the motion picture production of that name and manages the Micheaux Book and Film Company at 8 South Dearborn street. When the play *The Homesteader* played to big crowds at the Eighth Regiment Armory the "know-alls" predicted it had run its course in Chicago. Quite to the contrary, it has filled fourteen other engagements on the South Side and the show houses are clamoring for its return. This is by far the best motion picture yet written, acted and staged by a Colored man. It deserves all the loyal support the race has given it.

Howard A. Phelps, "Negro Life in Chicago," *Half-Century Magazine* 6, No. 5 (May 1919): 14

OSCAR MICHEAUX   Unless one has some connection with the actual production of a photo play, it is impossible to fully recognize the tremendous scope which the motion picture embraces. The complete picture is a miniature replica of life, and all the varied forces which help to make life so complex, the intricate studies and problems of human nature, all enter into the physical makeup of the most lowly photo play.

The mastery, therefore, of the art of production, for indeed it is an art, is no small attainment, and success can only be assured when assisted by the most active encouragement and financial backing. The colored has dared to step into a world which has hitherto remained closed to him. His entrance into this unexplored field, is for him, terribly difficult. He is united in his themes, in obtaining casts that present genuine ability, and in his financial resources. He requires encouragement and assistance. He is the new-born babe who must be fondled until he can stand on his own feet, and if the race has any pride in presenting its own achievements in this field, it behooves it to interest itself, and morally encourage such efforts.

I do not wish anyone to construe this as a request for the suppression of criticism. Honest, intelligent criticism is an aid to the progress of any effort. The producer who has confidence in his ideals, solicits constructive criticism. But he also asks fairness, and fairness in criticism demands a familiarity with the aims of the producer, and a knowledge of the circumstances under which his efforts were materialized.

I have been informed that my last production, *Birthright*, has occasioned much adverse criticism, during its exhibition in Philadelphia. Newspapermen have denounced me as a colored Judas, merely because they were either unaware of my aims, or were not in sympathy with them. What then, are my aims, to which such critics have taken exception?

I have always tried to make my photo plays present the truth, to lay before the race a cross section of its own life, to view the colored heart from close range. My results might have been narrow at times, due perhaps to certain limited situations, which I endeavored to portray, but in those limited situations, the truth was the predominant characteristic. It is only by presenting those portions of the race portrayed in my pictures, in the light and background of their true state, that we can raise our people to greater heights. I am too much imbued with the spirit of Booker T. Washington to engraft false virtues upon ourselves, to make ourselves that which we are not. Nothing could be a greater blow to our own progress.

The recognition of our true situation, will react in itself as a stimulus for self-advancement.

It is these ideals that I have injected into my pictures, and which are now being criticized. Possibly my aims have been misunderstood, but criticism arising from such misunderstanding, only doubles the already overburdening labors of the colored producer.

If I have been retarded by the unjust criticism from my own race, it has been amply made up by the aid of the Royal Theatre, which from the very beginning, has encouraged the production of colored photo plays, and in the face of burning criticism, has continued to foster my aims, and help place my organization on a strong footing.

It is only by constructive criticism, arising from an intelligent understanding of the real problem, however, that the colored producer can succeed in his efforts and produce photo plays, that will not only be a credit to the race, but be on par with those of the white producer.

Oscar Micheaux, *Philadelphia Afro-American* (24 January 1925), cited in Henry T. Sampson, *Blacks in Black and White* (Metuchen, NJ: Scarecrow Press, 1977), pp. 53–55

DONALD BOGLE   Micheaux used the same techniques in promoting and financing his films that he had used with his books. But he had a new dash and flair, befitting a motion-picture director. A hefty six-footer, given to wearing long Russian coats and extravagant wide-brimmed hats, Micheaux is said to have toured the country, stepping out of cars and into meeting halls as if "he were God about to deliver a sermon." "Why, he was so impressive and so charming," said Lorenzo Tucker, one of the most important of Micheaux's leading men, "that he could talk the shirt off your back." Just this sort of charm enabled Micheaux to persuade Southern theater owners to show his films. On his tours, Micheaux approached white Southerners and told them of the new black audience. At first they shied away, but when he spoke of the cash register, theater managers listened. It was soon arranged to have Micheaux features shown at special matinee performances held for black audiences. His movies were also sometimes shown at midnight performances for white audiences eager for black camp. Aware of the mystique of black nightclubs, he inserted into his films cabaret scenes that would appeal to whites.

As for his actors, Micheaux generally gathered them from black acting companies such as the Lafayette Players in New York. But he came across some of his stars under bizarre circumstances. Legend has it that Micheaux would spot a figure or note a gesture or be struck by the way the light fell across a face and would immediately sign the person up. Lorenzo Tucker said he was first spotted by Micheaux in Philadelphia. Having gone there to audition for a show, he was sitting in the lobby of the Dunbar Hotel when crafty Micheaux, whom he did not know, approached him and asked if he was an actor. "You're one of them who *thinks* they are," Micheaux added. Afterward, Tucker went to see Micheaux in New York. He was given a part, and all in all worked in some fourteen Micheaux productions.

Micheaux cast his actors on the basis of type. He modeled his stars after white Hollywood personalities and publicized them as black versions. Handsome and smooth Lorenzo Tucker was first referred to as the "black Valentino." Later when talkies came in, he was the "colored William Powell." Sexy and insolent Bee Freeman, a vamp figure, was the "sepia Mae West." Slick Chester, a character actor who played gangster roles, was the "colored Cagney." Lovely Ethel Moses was sometimes touted as the "Negro Harlow." The leads in Micheaux pictures were usually played by light-colored Negro actors, and in later years Micheaux was to be severely criticized by more militant black audiences for selecting "light-brights."

Once Micheaux had completed a film, he carried stills from it to theater managers. "Here's my black Valentino. The girls love him," he would boast. "If I can get the right backing, I'll star him in my next film, too." In this way he was often able to solicit financing for his *next* picture. He also sent his stars on personal-appearance junkets to Northern ghetto theaters. By these vigorous promotion tactics he established himself as the most successful black moviemaker of the period.

Donald Bogle, *Toms, Coons, Mulattoes, Mammies, and Bucks: An Interpretive History of Blacks in American Films* (New York: Continuum, 1973 [rev. ed. 1989]), pp. 111–14

DANIEL J. LEAB   Micheaux initially received high praise from the black press for his endeavors and his enterprise ⟨in filmmaking⟩. But in time critics began to take him to task for his depiction of the life of the black community. As early as 1920 Lester Walton, though he praised a Micheaux movie called *The Brute* (starring the black prizefighter Sam Langford), commented at length on the scenes of crap games, black dives, wife-beating, and women congregating to gamble. These scenes, Wilcox said, were "not any too pleasing to those of us who desire to see the better side of Negro life portrayed"; they reminded him of "the attitude of the daily press, which magnifies our vices and minimizes our virtues." In 1925 Sylvester Russell of the Pittsburgh *Courier* reported on his arguments with Micheaux about "the objectionable race features" in the producer's films. Other black newspapers also criticized Micheaux, but seemingly their objections made little impression on him.

Although Micheaux could and did ignore his critics in the black press, he could not disregard his film company's deteriorating financial condition. The return on even the most successful black film was relatively small. There were about 20,000 movie theaters in the United States in 1926, but only a few hundred of these would play an all-black production, and theaters that catered to ghetto audiences charged reduced admission prices. Even if one includes the Southern theaters that had special midnight showings for blacks, the potential earnings were severely limited. And rarely did a black producer reach all the possible exhibitors, given his necessarily makeshift system of distribution. Micheaux was a clever businessman, but he was no exception.

Moreover, the novelty of the all-black movie was beginning to wear thin. In 1917 the New York *Age,* although acknowledging the drawbacks of a Douglass company movie, still praised it as "a racial business venture which ought to be encouraged." But, already by 1920 the *Age* was pointing out that "the day of expecting charitable consideration in business even of our own people just because we are Negroes is past." Though Micheaux's films did improve technically, they still remained amateurish by comparison with Hollywood's products. Ghetto audiences began to stay away from "race productions," and as one black newspaperman noted, "the worst enemy of the race production is the race movie fan himself." In February 1928, the Micheaux Film Corporation filed a voluntary petition of bankruptcy. It should be noted that Micheaux, ever the careful businessman, had seen to it that most of the corporation's films were legally the property of his wife.

Oscar Micheaux's silent motion picture works cannot be considered outstanding. He is significant, however, because he was one of the first independent black producers making popular and for a time profitable movies with black actors and actresses for ghetto audiences. Despite his public utterances, Micheaux's films were not designed to uplift or to enlighten. They were meant to entertain, to appeal to his concept of black popular taste, and to make money.

Daniel J. Leab, *From Sambo to Superspade: The Black Experience in Motion Pictures* (Boston: Houghton Mifflin, 1975), pp. 79–81

ARLENE ELDER   Micheaux's story of his life on the South Dakota Prairie is doubly significant. First, it represents an American ideal at the turn of the century—the movement west and the opening up of the country. More interesting for the student of cultural pluralism, however, is Micheaux's self-conscious emotional division between personal ambition, marked by intense frontier individualism, and his hope of being not only a racial representative but a leader of his people and a model for them. Reflective of this paradoxical self-image is the contrast he establishes between the City and the Wilderness as he develops his theme of the West. This symbolic juxtaposition also serves as the organizing principle for his discussion of race.

Like the writings of other regionalists, Micheaux's books provide a wealth of topographical, historical, and political information. He gives details about the methods of holding lotteries to settle the country (first choice of a homesite going to the holder of the first number pulled from a pile by a blindfolded child); the astonishing way new towns sprang up almost over-night on the prairie; and the way two-story buildings in the town which boomed a few months before would be sawn in half and both parts moved to the next settlement boosted by the local businessmen, who had themselves started from nothing and flourished overnight. He enlightens us on the condition of the Indians, especially the social history of families of "breeds" like the Amoureaux who were ranchers, owners of great herds of cattle and much land, and "high moguls in little Crow society." He emphasizes the importance of the railroad in making or breaking the fortunes of the towns and farms in its path; and he skillfully describes the appearance and unusual features of the new country, frequently described as "the hollow of God's hand." Despite Micheaux's interest in local color, however, his real subject is himself. The introduction to his autobiography 〈*The Conquest*〉 states: "This is a true story of a negro who was discontented and the circumstances that were the outcome of that discontent."

Arlene Elder, "Oscar Micheaux: The Melting Pot on the Plains," *Old Northwest* 2, No. 3 (September 1976): 299–300

THOMAS CRIPPS   Nearly all of Micheaux's films are lost. If one of the silent pictures must stand for his canon it would be *Body and Soul* (1924), both for what it said and for the response it evoked. The picture represented the highest level of achievement for Micheaux. For the first time he wrestled with the nature of the black community, without recourse to shoddy devices, overdressing in the good cloth of Dunbar or Chesnutt, or interracial sensationalism. The theme allowed full play to his racial consciousness. To his stable of new stars he added Paul Robeson, fresh from triumphs on the white man's stage and football fields at Rutgers. The result was a rich black imagery that never materialized in other survivals of the 1920s and a modest accommodation with black intellectuals. For years black leaders, including Booker T. Washington, had railed against "jackleg" preachers who exploited the deep religiosity of poor blacks who settled in cold ghettos and turned to the charismatic churches as visible proof that their old Southern rural lives still had meaning. In *Body and Soul* Micheaux not only exposed cultist parasites but also advertised the promise that blacks could organize against the bootleggers and gamblers in their midst.

Not that Micheaux worked out all the themes in lonely isolation. To the contrary, his first print submitted to the New York censor board presented the preacher as the embodiment of unredeemed evil, with not a single redemptive quality in the black community. The New York censors would not tolerate it for much the same reason the NAACP would have given. So Micheaux recut it and fabricated an elaborate and confusing sequence which allowed the ingenue to awake and find that the preacher was a covert spy assigned to break up a bootlegging ring. If blacks could make movies in isolation, they still could not release them until white eyes had approved them. Furthermore, whites seemed to have developed a sensitivity to racial slurs that escaped the cavalier Micheaux.

The second version, bearing white fingermarks, may have given rounded dimensions to Negro life. The balance demanded by the censor board broadened the scope of the conflict and forced the characters into protagonist-antagonist tension. In the case of Paul Robeson's preacher, it enlarged the role into complex parts. In a dual role he brought power to the gambler's cynical smile and to the preacher's practical piety. Micheaux gave him tight closeups that tilted up to capture a virility long missing from black figures. Robeson fairly oozed the strength and sexuality of enthusiastic religion while at the same time giving off the hard, ominous energy of the "bad nigger" gambler. For Robeson, it was one of the few occasions when he cut free of white direction and bridged the deep fissure in the black world between the venal, erotic Staggerlee and respectable black bourgeois. His power carried him above the necessarily confused plot and allowed him to make a sensitive measurement of black character in American life.

Micheaux too reached high. In spite of the stagey, unmatched cutaway shots inherent in low-budget shooting, the garbled plot, and the broad comedy relief, he pulled off a modestly successful black movie. The exteriors had the rough and unpainted texture of Auburn Avenue, Beale Street, or some other black Southern promenade. The sets reinforced the dichotomy of the roles with simplistic, yet effective tricks. In the main saloon set a *Police Gazette* cover gazed down like a broad wink, while a benign portrait of Booker T. Washington set the tone of bourgeois ambience in the ingenue's home. In the end Micheaux contrived his way around the New York censor board by shifting Robeson from venal preacher to cool detective, at once tricking the audience into expecting a white man's "bad nigger," and symbolically turning away from the hoary stereotype. ⟨. . .⟩

There is no way of knowing whether *Body and Soul* revived the black cinema movement, but it surely arrived coincident with sanguine conditions. By the mid-twenties black communities had become better organized and more self-conscious, and the movies reflected the new awareness. Micheaux not only survived the decade but increased the social thrust of his pictures. His *Spider's Web* (1926) treated the love-hate relationship between the ghetto and the "numbers game"; *The Wages of Sin* (1929) analyzed the strains of urban life upon the black family; *Birthright* (1924) followed a Negro Ivy Leaguer southward to minister to his people's needs. Gradually the translucent watermarks of the middle-class ideologies of personal aspiration and of black solidarity tinged his films.

> Thomas Cripps, *Slow Fade to Black: The Negro in American Film 1900–1942* (New York: Oxford University Press, 1977), pp. 191–93

CHARLES J. FONTENOT, JR.   Not only was Micheaux the first black writer to portray a black leading character in the role of a pioneer, he was also the first black film maker. He produced at least forty-five movies and organized private corporations to distribute both his films and his books. Micheaux tried to present a realistic picture of black urban life in contrast to that which then emanated from Hollywood studios. Instead of emphasizing the carnal or gutter instinct of black people, he tried to portray the problems of the black middle class. Although he has been criticized for casting light-skinned people as actors in his films, for imitating white society, and for using black people as plastic models, he sought to offer meaningful alternatives to the negative images created by the American film industry. ⟨. . .⟩

Although Micheaux operated independently, a good many of his critics seek to equate his productions with those Hollywood made for blacks. Eileen Landry writes that Micheaux's stories were "often typically Hollywood— adventures, melodramas, mysteries—starring black actors. There was little 'ethnic truth' to these films; Micheaux gave his audiences a 'black Valentino' and a 'sepia Mae West.' And he perpetuated many white stereotypes; his heroes and heroines were usually light-skinned and fine-featured, his villains darker and more negroid. While some of his films dealt with the problem of being black, this was never from the point of view of the ghetto dweller or sharecropper; his subjects were the black bourgeoisie."

The same sort of comments have been made by those among Micheaux's critics who fail to place his books and films within the parameters of his conscious intention. Such criticism also omits from consideration the strongest characters Micheaux created—black pioneers. For it was through the creation of the black pioneer as an individual able to collapse the distinction between race and class that Micheaux made his most lasting contribution to black literature and films. The black pioneer is freed from the artifices of "civilization" and is allowed to fulfill his own potential through a process inherent in his cultural history.

Oscar Micheaux is emblematic of the black pioneer as a symbol of black achievement. The character was derived from experiences he himself had lived through. His films explore various aspects of the problem of being black in a racially oriented society from the point of view of black goal-oriented behavior. Central to the mythology he constructed in his novels and popularized in his films is the emphasis on abandoning metropolitan black areas and moving to the Great Northwest, where black men and women could build a civilization based on their own cultural ethos. Micheaux's impact on black film is widely recognized, even though its nature is debated. His film making stands as a symbol of the race pride he sought to instill in black people through his emphasis on the values of the black middle class.

> Charles J. Fontenot, Jr., "Oscar Micheaux, Black Novelist and Film Maker," *Vision and Refuge: Essays on the Literature of the Great Plains*, ed. Virginia Faulkner and Frederick C. Luebke (Lincoln: Center for Great Plains Studies/University of Nebraska Press, 1982), pp. 109–10, 123–24

JOSEPH A. YOUNG   Utilizing the pathos of his own provocative experiences as a Black in early twentieth-century Jim Crow America, Oscar Micheaux fought the cause of individual emancipation by publishing novels that reflect, with minor alterations, the black stereotypes of the post-bellum confederate romanticists: the best of the cavalier racists (Joel Harris and Thomas Page) as well as the worst of the Negrophobes (Thomas Dixon). Micheaux assumed that by adopting the world view of both the proslavery imperialist and the imperialist of industrial expansion, he could escape the humiliating and impotent status typically allotted to the Afro-American and be free to follow the American dream. But such a scheme follows an ambivalent and a dubious line of reasoning. To adopt the world view of the oppressor requires him to reject blackness, that is, to reject both his racial kinsmen and himself. Micheaux, like other black writers of the assimilationist school, idealistically assumed that assimilation of black and white cultures would occur only if Blacks could pass for white; or, if passing for white was a cosmetic impossibility, Blacks could become fit for American culture by adopting Anglo-Saxon myths, Anglo-Saxon values, and Anglo-Saxon philosophy. ⟨. . .⟩

The importance of Micheaux is not so much in his literary achievements, but in his unwitting illustration of how oppressive myths have been forced on Blacks, especially black novelists who as artists should have been writing in the finest tradition of Western humanism or of a truly black aesthetic philosophy, earnestly attempting to answer the questions, "Who are we?" and "What is life all about?" Addison Gayle in *The Way of the New World* argues that the shortcoming of many black novelists of the past—and even of the present—is in their not having adopted this ideological voice: that the images, metaphors, and symbols that nurture a sense of self-importance and achievement have been created and controlled, manipulated and defined by outsiders. Without this voice or this focus, the mental oppression initiated originally to strip enslaved Africans of their humanity continues.

Micheaux did not address the question, "What is life all about?" Instead, he wrote novels that looked back to the Age of Accommodation and Reconciliation in which Blacks were forced to assume the role of "darky" or "brute," becoming the scapegoat and the butt for the country's frustrations in its attempt to pacify differences between its regional and ethnic white minorities after civil war. Arguably, Micheaux presupposed that the only avenue to success in such a Jim Crow climate would be to use the myth of black inferiority and try to shape it, make it flexible for his personal success. Micheaux became, therefore, an apologist for Booker T. Washington's accommodating strategies and for American imperialism in the hope of gaining material wealth and marginal acceptance. He accepted black folk's position as definitive and as permanently outside or at the bottom of the political, social, and economic mainstream of America. He condemned Blacks to perpetual third-class citizenship, holding them responsible for their condition. And he used the pseudoscience of craniology to dismiss the majority of Blacks as genetically inferior. But Micheaux also suggested that some Blacks could be redeemed if they would follow the teachings and emulate the example of his property-minded, Nietzschean superman hero.

If they would migrate west, acquire property, build up capital, and participate in settling the country, this group would in time be saved, or at least be assimilated.

> Joseph A. Young, "Introduction," *Black Novelist as White Racist: The Myth of Black Inferiority in the Novels of Oscar Micheaux* (Westport, CT: Greenwood Press, 1989), pp. ix–xi

⧉ *Bibliography*

Books:

The Conquest: The Story of a Negro Pioneer. 1913.

The Forged Note: A Romance of the Darker Races. 1915.

The Homesteader. 1917.

The Wind from Nowhere. 1941.

The Case of Mrs. Wingate. 1944.

The Story of Dorothy Stanfield, Based on a Great Insurance Swindle, and a Woman! 1946.

The Masquerade: An Historical Novel. 1947.

Films:

Circumstancial Evidence. 1920.

Within Our Gates. 1920.

The Gunsaulus Mystery. 1921.

The Hypocrite. 1921.

The Shadow. 1921.

Symbol of the Unconquered ⟨The Wilderness Trail⟩. 1921.

The Dungeon. 1922.

The Homesteader. 1922.

Uncle Jasper's Will ⟨Jasper Landry's Will⟩. 1922.

Deceit. 1923.

The Ghost of Tolston's Manor. 1923.

The Virgin of Seminole. 1923.

Birthright. 1924.

A Son of Satan. 1924.

Body and Soul. 1925.

The Brute. 1925.

Marcus Garland. 1925.

The Conjure Woman. 1926.

The Devil's Disciple. 1926.

The Broken Violin. 1927.

The House Behind the Cedars. 1927.

The Millionaire. 1927.

The Spider's Web. 1927.

Thirty Years Later. 1928.

When Men Betray. 1928.

Wages of Sin. 1929.

Daughter of the Congo. 1930.

Easy Street. 1930.

Darktown Review. 1931.

The Exile. 1931.

Black Magic. 1932.

Ten Minutes to Live. 1932.

Veiled Aristocrats. 1932.

The Girl from Chicago. 1933.

Ten Minutes to Kill. 1933.

Harlem After Midnight. 1934.

Len Hawkin's Confession. 1935.

Swing. 1936.

Temptation. 1936.

Underworld. 1937.

Miracle in Harlem. 1937.

God's Stepchildren. 1939.

Birthright. 1939.

Lying Lips. 1939.

The Notorious Elinor Lee. 1940.

The Betrayal. 1948.

Phillis Wheatley

c. 1753–1784

PHILLIS WHEATLEY'S exact birthdate is unknown, but it is estimated at 1753 or 1754. She was possibly born in Senegal. It is certain that Wheatley arrived, in bondage, in New England in 1761. She was purchased by John Wheatley—from whom she took her surname—as a present for his wife Susanna. She was a precocious child who, according to her biographer, William H. Robinson, mastered the English language in sixteen months. Phillis soon acquired the fundamentals of a classical education, becoming acquainted with the Bible as well as a good deal of English literature and Greek and Latin literature in translation. She also learned Latin. The Wheatleys, who were proud of Phillis, introduced her to the affluent and educated circles of Boston society, where she was received warmly for her erudition and charm, and also for the fact that she was an educated slave— a rarity, and some thought an impossibility, in the Boston of that day.

Wheatley's *An Elegiac Poem, on the Death of That Celebrated Divine, and Eminent Servant of Jesus Christ, the Reverend and Learned George Whitefield* (1770) was her first separate publication, though it is thought that she wrote many poems earlier than 1770, such as "On Being Brought from Africa to America" and "To the University of Cambridge, in New England," some of which appeared in various periodicals. "On Messrs. Hussey and Coffin," published in the *Newport Mercury* for 1767, is her first known appearance in print.

Wheatley's elegy on George Whitefield garnered much attention because of the popularity of the evangelist and because of the delicately crafted lines in which he was celebrated. Yet it was the publication of *Poems on Various Subjects, Religious and Moral* (1773) that solidified her reputation as a poet. Just before its publication in England, Wheatley was received with fascination and hospitality in London society under the sponsorship of the Countess of Huntingdon, to whom Wheatley dedicated the collection. The voyage to England provided a strong draft of freedom for Wheatley, and some

119

speculate that she was freed as early as a month after her return, but certainly by 1778.

Poems on Various Subjects is marked by a strong neoclassical influence. Alexander Pope, perhaps Wheatley's favorite poet, is especially reflected in the carefully wrought lines, use of the heroic couplet, highly restrained, impersonal tone, and classical allusions. Wheatley's familiarity with the Bible is also evident in her verse, especially in her numerous elegies. She is often criticized for not addressing the position of her race in colonial society, but this was not Wheatley's focus. She did, however, follow political events: many of her occasional poems were inspired by the early flickers and later flames of revolution. This is reflected by her poetic appeals to such men as King George III (1768), the Earl of Dartmouth (1772), and George Washington (1775), and titles such as *Liberty and Peace* (1784). Yet political events so overshadowed interest in her poetry that her publications became less frequent after 1773.

Phillis Wheatley moved with her master John Wheatley to Providence in 1775 but returned to Boston after the British evacuation in 1776. After the death of John Wheatley on March 12, 1778, Phillis married John Peters, a free black Bostonian with whom she had three children. The marriage proved to be an unhappy one marked by financial difficulties. Phillis Wheatley died, apparently abandoned by her husband, in a boarding house on December 5, 1784.

◈ *Critical Extracts*

THOMAS JEFFERSON   Misery is often the parent of the most affecting touches in poetry. Among the blacks is misery enough, God knows, but no poetry. ⟨. . .⟩ Religion, indeed, has produced a Phyllis Whately; but it could not produce a poet. The compositions published under her name are below the dignity of criticism.

> Thomas Jefferson, *Notes on the State of Virginia* (1784), *Basic Writings*, ed. Philip S. Foner (Garden City, NY: Halcyon House, 1950), p. 146

G. HERBERT RENFRO   Having learned to read, Phillis readily learned to write, her own curiosity prompting to it, as her master testified.

Possessing at first no writing materials, her genius improvised some for the occasion. Not being supplied with pen and paper, she found ever-ready substitutes in a piece of chalk or charcoal and brick wall. In this and other ways indicating unusual ability, much attention was directed to her from the Wheatley household. That excellent family soon learned that, instead of obtaining a spirit born to serve, there had come among them a spirit born to create. In her twelfth year Phillis was able to carry on an extensive correspondence on the most important and interesting topics of the day with many of the wisest and most learned in Boston and London. Having mastered the English language within the short period of four years she began the study of the Latin tongue, and her progress in this was only paralleled by her remarkable record in the study of English. She soon made a translation of one of Ovid's tales. It was considered so admirable for one so young, and so extraordinary for one of the African race, that friends insisted on its publication. The translation was received with great favor, and on her visit to England, a few years later, it was republished, calling forth many encomiums from the public press.

The news of such progress, made even in the large city of Boston by an unknown African slave, could not be concealed. Public attention was directed toward her. Friends of the Wheatleys, refined and intelligent, came to visit the African prodigy, to witness her proficiency, and to cultivate her friendship. Thus becoming acquainted with many of the best people of Boston, she was often invited to their homes, and, during these visits, mindful of the prejudice against her race, she always conducted herself in so becoming a manner, while a recipient of honors, as to give no offense to the most prejudiced mind whom accident or design might cause her to meet on these occasions.

The city of Boston was even then the intellectual metropolis of the New World, having within her confines a numerous class of men distinguished for their literary attainments. Yet, education was not so widely disseminated as to be regarded as universal. The illiteracy of the master was often covered by the pride of his station, but that of the slave was exposed to the sunlight. Hence, we can account in a measure for the indulgence shown to Phillis, and the curiosity excited by her efforts. Here was a slave girl, just entering upon her teens, whose entire education was gathered from private instruction of a few years at her master's house, who was able to converse and discuss with the most learned and cultivated people of Boston; many of whom sought her society, loaned her books, gave her encouragement, acknowledged her merit and respected her abilities. Nor is this the first occasion in history that the wise and intelligent have found worth and merit in the conversation and virtues of a child.

G. Herbert Renfro, "A Sketch of the Life of Phillis Wheatley," *Life and Works of Phillis Wheatley* (Washington, DC: Robert L. Pendleton, 1916), pp. 11–12

JAMES WELDON JOHNSON   Phillis Wheatley's poetry is the poetry of the Eighteenth Century. She wrote when Pope and Gray were supreme; it is easy to see that Pope was her model. Had she come under the influence of Wordsworth, Byron or Keats or Shelley, she would have done greater work. As it is, her work must not be judged by the work and standards of a later day, but by the work and standards of her own day and her own contemporaries. By this method of criticism she stands out as one of the important characters in the making of American literature, without any allowances for her sex or antecedents. ⟨. . .⟩

⟨. . .⟩ Only very seldom does Phillis Wheatley sound a native note. Four times in single lines she refers to herself as "Afric's muse." In a poem of admonition addressed to the students at the "University of Cambridge in New England" she refers to herself as follows:

> Ye blooming plants of human race divine,
> An Ethiop tells you 'tis your greatest foe.

But one looks in vain for some outburst or even complaint against the bondage of her people, for some agonizing cry about her native land. In two poems she refers definitely to Africa as her home, but in each instance there seems to be under the sentiment of the lines a feeling of almost smug contentment at her own escape therefrom. ⟨. . .⟩

What Phillis Wheatley failed to achieve is due in no small degree to her education and environment. Her mind was steeped in the classics; her verses are filled with classical and mythological allusions. She knew Ovid thoroughly and was familiar with other Latin authors. She must have known Alexander Pope by heart. And, too, she was reared and sheltered in a wealthy and cultured family,—a wealthy and cultured Boston family; she never had the opportunity to learn life; she never found out her own true relation to life and to her surroundings. And it should not be forgotten that she was only about thirty years old when she died. The impulsion or the compulsion that might have driven her genius off the worn paths, out on a journey of exploration, Phillis Wheatley never received. But, whatever her limitations, she merits more than America has accorded her.

James Weldon Johnson, "Preface," *The Book of American Negro Poetry* (New York: Harcourt, Brace & World, 1922), pp. 25, 28–29, 31

BENJAMIN BRAWLEY   *Poems on Various Subjects* lists thirty-eight titles, aside from "A Rebus by I. B.," to which one of the pieces is a reply. Fourteen of the poems are elegiac, and at least six others were called forth by special occasions. Two are paraphrases from the Bible. We are thus left with sixteen poems to represent the best that Phillis Wheatley had produced by the time she was twenty years old. One of the longest of these is "Niobe in Distress for Her Children Slain by Apollo, from Ovid's Metamorphoses, Book VI, and from a View of the Painting of Mr. Richard Wilson." This contains two interesting examples of personification neither of which seems to be drawn from Ovid, "fate portentous whistling in the air" and "the feather'd vengeance quiv'ring in his hands," though the point might be easily made that these are but the stock-in-trade of pseudo-classicism. "To S. M., a Young African Painter, on Seeing His Works" was addressed to Scipio Moorhead, servant of the Reverend John Moorhead, who exhibited some talent with the brush and one of whose subjects was the friendship of Damon and Pythias. The early poem, "On Being Brought from Africa to America," consisting of only eight lines, is one of the few pieces with autobiographical interest, and there is also a reference to race in the lines addressed to William, Earl of Dartmouth; but in general Phillis Wheatley is abstract, polite, restrained. "An Hymn to Humanity" is one of the most conventional pieces in the volume. One can but speculate upon what the author might have done if she had lived to see the French Revolution and to feel the glow of romanticism of Wordsworth and Coleridge and Scott.

Yet, when all discount is made, when we have spoken of the influence of Pope and of the few examples of lyrical expression, we are still forced to wonder at the ease with which the young author, technically a slave, could chisel the heroic couplet. Her achievement in this line is as amazing as it is unique.

Benjamin Brawley, *The Negro Genius* (New York: Dodd, Mead, 1937), pp. 25–27

JULIAN D. MASON, JR.   It is quite clear that Phillis Wheatley was not a great poet. She was not a poet in the classical Greek sense of maker, seer, creator, nor were her concerns really with Emerson's meter making argument or Poe's rhythmical creation of beauty. Phillis Wheatley had aspirations, but she also knew her shortcomings; and her concerns were less august, less pretentious. Her primary endeavor was to put into rhythmical, poetic forms those thoughts which came to her or which were brought to her attention by the small crises and significant experiences of the people of Boston as they met life and death from day to day. Most of what she wrote of was not noted by the world outside of that city, though she occasionally did treat more general topics and there is some evidence that before and after the Revolution her poetic horizons may have been broadening.

On the basis of the poems which have survived her short career, she must be labelled as primarily an occasional poet, one interested in the clever crafting of verse. Such a craftsman is not as concerned with selecting topics and creating patterns as with taking a given or obvious topic and fitting it skillfully to an already existing pattern. However, if he is a good craftsman, he is distinctive in his own right and possesses a great gift which is worthy of the world's attention, if not its lasting praise. Such was Phillis Wheatley's gift and her concern, as she was a better craftsman of verse than most of the others attempting the same type of thing in America in the 1770's, a time and place which certainly produced more craftsmen than true poets. Her reward was in immediate praise—not the type which echoes through the ages, but which appropriately sounds again from time to time for only brief periods.

Julian D. Mason, Jr., "Introduction," *The Poems of Phillis Wheatley* (Chapel Hill: University of North Carolina Press, 1966), pp. xx–xxi

---

M. A. RICHMOND   The crowning legacy of the poet's time in London was a volume of her verse, the first book by a black woman to be published. It was entitled *Poems on Various Subjects, Religious and Moral* and dedicated to her patron, Selina Shirley (Lady Huntingdon). Her ladyship graciously permitted the dedication, and for this dispensation the poet and her mistress were effusive in their gratitude.

The poet's thanks included a shrewd calculation and a jolting lapse from her literary style. "Under the patronage of your Ladyship," she wrote, ". . . my feeble efforts will be shielded from the severe trials of uppity Criticism. . . ." Uppity?

If one realizes that the Wheatley volume, appearing more than a century and a half after the first pilgrim landing at Plymouth, was still among the first volumes of verse by a colonist to be published, one may appreciate how rare a phenomenon it was. For a woman slave, barely turned twenty, it was a dazzling triumph. The gift of the black slave could not be placed on the market without a white testimonial that it was genuine.

Appended to the volume was a statement by eighteen prestigious residents of Boston, attesting to its authenticity. Among the eighteen were Thomas Hutchinson, royal governor of Massachusetts Colony; James Bowdoin, who was to be governor of the state of Massachusetts; John Hancock, possessor of the most celebrated signature in American history; and seven ministers. Men of substance all, conscious of it, affixing their valuable signatures to the ponderously drawn affadavit designed to impress even the most skeptical with its judicious restraint. It was a strange introduction to poetry:

> We, whose names are under-written, do assure the World, that the Poems specified in the following Page were, (as we verily believe) written by Phillis, a young Negro Girl, who was but a few years since, brought an uncultivated barbarian, from Africa, and has ever since been, and now is, under the disadvantage of serving as a slave in a Family in this Town. She has been examined by some of the best Judges, and is thought qualified to write them.

M. A. Richmond, *Bid the Vassal Soar: Interpretative Essays on the Life and Poetry of Phillis Wheatley and George Moses Horton* (Washington, DC: Howard University Press, 1974), pp. 33–34

MUKHTAR ALI ISANI   Phillis Wheatley not only gained her initial fame with an elegy, the celebrated poem on George Whitefield's death in 1770, but over the remaining years of her life retained her place in the public eye in no small part because of her facility with the elegy. A third of her compositions in *Poems on Various Subjects, Religious and Moral* (1773) are elegies. Elegies appear in like proportion among the poems she tried in vain to publish as her second collection, in 1779. She received little recognition as an elegist, but these poems have merit. They make effective use of the mix of elegiac traditions prevailing in the poet's time. While they are comparatively numerous, they are genuine effusions of a feeling heart. While they appear to be composed with rapidity and sometimes even in haste, they are generally the result of careful planning and thoughtful revision. Their faults are obvious but their strengths must also be noted. Certainly, these poems lent her much of her contemporaneous fame. ⟨. . .⟩

More than personal piety is responsible for the religious flavor of Wheatley's poems. The influence of the tradition of the New England funeral elegy is especially evident. By Wheatley's time, the funeral elegy, once the prerogative of the clerics, was almost entirely the work of laymen, including those with no special call to letters. Broadsides remained in vogue, but increasingly such verse was appearing through the cheaper media of newspapers and magazines. The didactic emphasis and the use of mortuary detail continued, but the latter was declining. Wheatley's use of pentameter couplets and emphatic mortuary reminders is in the tradition of the New England funerary verse. Current practice was responsible for encouraging the use of the stock image and phrase. The recurring personification of Death, the frequent return to "the mansions of the dead," the visions of spirits, and the sounds of angelic choirs had the sanction of the time. Occasionally, the poet can be accused of sentimentalism, but the neoclassic restraint which was changing the tone of the Puritan elegy was also an influence on Wheatley's poetry.

In its choice of elements and in its emphasis, Wheatley's elegiac verse bears a stamp of its own. The poet set up a pattern and, unfortunately, often repeated herself. Her typical elegy is not principally a song of sorrow. It is a poem of solace through praise. It often relies on dialog to achieve *anagnorisis*. Its setting is not in this world but in the next, and its comfort is based on the pious philosophy that the world to come is a happier place than man's terrestrial home.

> Mukhtar Ali Isani, "Phillis Wheatley and the Elegiac Mode," *Critical Essays on Phillis Wheatley*, ed. William H. Robinson (Boston: G. K. Hall, 1982), pp. 208–10

WILLIAM H. ROBINSON   It is true that practically all of her writings are informed by a lifelong preoccupation with orthodox Christian piety. But that fundamental fact will not form the basis for deducing that her range was limited to Christian or Biblical or even pious concerns. Phillis composed over one hundred poems and published more than fifty pieces in her lifetime, certainly enough to display a wider range of topics than that for which she has been credited. In the thirty-eight pieces in her 1773 volume alone can be seen pieces on such matters as reconciliation, "the works of Providence," delightful companion lyrics of the Morning and the Evening, two Biblical renderings, a Latin translation, a tribute to a fellow black Bostonian who was also a poet and an artist, the human imagination. Most of these pieces are, however, variously structured elegies, versified comfortings for recent widows, widowers, parents grieving the death of their children or relatives.

In poems published before and after the 1773 volume, her range of poetic concerns includes topics of American patriotism, simple friendship, pioneering tributes to black Africa. Indications of still other topics may be reckoned from some of the titles of the thirty-three poems listed in her proposals for a 1779 volume, a volume that was never published: "Thoughts on the Times," "Farewell to England," "Epithalamium to Mrs. H——," "A Complaint." Likewise, her letters reveal a lively interest in several issues: antislavery, her chronic sickness, her ordeals as a bookseller and distributor of her own book, her manumission, the onset of Christian redemption of "heathen" Africans. The charge that she versified nothing but piety cannot be documented.

She may have written heartfelt condolences for personal Tory friends, but Phillis was plainly a Whig or American Patriot in her deepest political sympathies. This much is clear in a half-dozen poems she wrote. One of her very first efforts, "America," is a versified, allegorical chiding of Mother England for the imposition of unduly inhibiting taxation on her vigorous, growing son, New England, or America. Hailing King George III for his repeal of the Stamp Act, so despised in the colonies and especially in Boston where it had triggered mob riots, Phillis wrote two versions of a poem of American thanks to his majesty. The Earl of Dartmouth was appreciated in some of the colonies as a sometimes sympathetic recourse for American grievances. Congratulating him on his royal appointment as Secretary of State for North America, she greets his "blissful sway," because

> No more, *America,* in mournful strain
> Of wrongs, and grievance unredress'd complain;
> Which wanton *Tyranny* with lawless hand
> Had made, and with it meant t'enslave the land.

She also took occasion in this piece to testify of her own experiences as a kidnapped African slave to underscore the great hope with which, she was sure, her fellow colonists must greet Dartmouth's tenure. As she was herself a slave or unpaid servant, however indulged, when she wrote this poem, the piece can easily be read as her disdain for all kinds of slavery.

William H. Robinson, "On Phillis Wheatley's Poetry," *Phillis Wheatley and Her Writings* (New York: Garland, 1984), pp. 91–92.

HENRY LOUIS GATES, JR.   Imitating Pope in rhythm and meter, Wheatley wrote in decasyllabic lines of closed heroic couplets. There is much use of invocation, hyperbole, and inflated ornamentation, and an overemphasis of personification, all of which characterize neoclassical poetry.

Seventeen, or one-third, of her extant poems are elegies, fourteen of which appeared in the first edition of *Poems on Various Subjects, Religious and Moral* and five of which have been revised from earlier published elegies. In one of the few close readings of Wheatley's verse, Gregory Rigsby demonstrates conclusively that her elegies are a creative variation of the "English Elegy" and the "Puritan Elegy." Wheatley's elegies are threnodic after the fashion of the "Renaissance Elegy," in that they are meant "to praise the subject, to lament the death, and to comfort the bereaved." Yet they are "Medieval" rather than "Elizabethan" insofar as they prefer a sublime resignation to an unrestrained death force, and seem to avoid the protest against it. The medieval resignation toward death, the function of the "Renaissance Elegy," and the form of the threnody as it developed in Elizabethan poetry were fused together in the "Puritan Funeral Elegy," a form peculiar to colonial America.

The Puritan funeral elegy, in turn, derived its specific shape and tone from the early American funeral sermon, based as it was on energetic exhortation. But, as Rigsby argues, Wheatley utilized the triple function of the Renaissance elegy within "her own elegiac structure and established more elaborate conventions." Rigsby then identifies these elements to be the underlying "structure of a Wheatley elegy": (1) the deceased in Heaven, (2) the deceased "winging" his way to Heaven, (3) an appreciation of the deceased's work on earth, (4) seraphic strains of heavenly bliss, (5) consolation of the living, (6) exhortation. The identification of the conventions of her elegies indicates that Wheatley was an imaginative artist to a degree largely unrecognized in critical literature. Although her remaining occasional verse lacks the irony, the contrast, and the balance of Pope's poetry, which she cited as her conscious model, her critical reception since the eighteenth century has failed in a remarkably consistent way to read her verse in comparison with the various literary traditions that she so obviously attempted to imitate and by which she just as obviously sought to measure herself. Curiously, all of her extant poems, except five, utilize the heroic couplet. Vernon Loggins traces, albeit vaguely, the influence of Milton in her hymns to morning and evening, as well as in her poem to General Lee, as he does Gray's influence on her elegy to Whitefield and Addison and Watt's presence in "Ode to Neptune" and "Hymn to Humanity." But these, again, are suggestions of influence rather than practical criticism.

Henry Louis Gates, Jr., "Phillis Wheatley and the 'Nature of the Negro,' " *Figures in Black: Words, Signs, and the "Racial" Self* (New York: Oxford University Press, 1987), pp. 78–79

HENRY LOUIS GATES, JR.   That the progenitor of the black
literary tradition was a woman means, in the most strictly literal sense, that
all subsequent black writers have evolved in a matrilinear line of descent,
and that each, consciously or unconsciously, has extended and revised a
canon whose foundation was the poetry of a black woman. Early black
writers seem to have been keenly aware of Wheatley's founding role, even
if most of her white reviewers were more concerned with the implications
of her race than her gender. Jupiter Hammon, for example, whose 1760
broadside "An Evening Thought. Salvation by Christ, With Penitential
Cries" was the first individual poem published by a black American, acknowledged Wheatley's influence by selecting her as the subject of his second
broadside, "An Address to Miss Phillis Wheatly [sic], Ethiopian Poetess, in
Boston," which was published at Hartford in 1778. And George Moses
Horton, the second Afro-American to publish a book of poetry in English
(1829), brought out in 1838 an edition of his *Poems by a Slave* bound
together with Wheatley's work. Indeed, for fifty-six years, between 1773
and 1829, when Horton published *The Hope of Liberty*, Wheatley was the
only black person to have published a book of imaginative literature in
English. So central was this black woman's role in the shaping of the Afro-
American literary tradition that, as one historian has maintained, the history
of the reception of Phillis Wheatley's poetry *is* the history of Afro-American
literary criticism. Well into the nineteenth-century, Wheatley and the black
literary tradition were the same entity.

> Henry Louis Gates, Jr., "Foreword: In Her Own Write," *The Collected Works of Phillis
> Wheatley*, ed. John C. Shields (New York: Oxford University Press, 1988), pp. x–xi

---

JOHN C. SHIELDS   Wheatley, who wrote most of her extant verse
by the age of twenty, has been censured for her alleged dependence on
and imitation of neoclassical conventions and poetics, and she has been
denigrated for lack of sympathy with her people's struggle for freedom. An
investigation of her poems and letters proves these charges false. In a letter
treating the slavery issue written in February 1774 and addressed to Samson
Occom, the American Indian Missionary, Wheatley forcefully and eloquently states, "In every human Brest, God has implanted a Principle, which
we call Love of Freedom; it is impatient of Oppression, and pants for
Deliverance." She made this statement some four months after her own
manumission. Not only was Wheatley vitally concerned for the plight of

her enslaved brothers and sisters, but she fervently sought her own freedom, both in this world and in the next. So complete was her absorption in the struggle for freedom that this endeavor governed her conception of poetry, causing her to be no more imitative than any other good student and writer of literature.

Wheatley articulates the theme of freedom in four ways. The first may be surprising, especially from the pen of a black slave: she sometimes uttered passionate political statements supporting the American colonial quest for freedom from Great Britain. Although not as readily observable, the second way is much more prevalent. Wheatley displays numerous examples of what Jung called the mandala archetype, a circular image pattern closely associated with a psychological attempt to discover freedom from chaos. The persistence of this pattern suggests Wheatley's discontent with her enslavement and indicates a means by which she adapted to it.

One conscious poetic escape from slavery was the writing of contemplative elegies; this was the third means by which Wheatley achieved freedom, not in this world but in the next. So enthusiastically does she celebrate death and its rewards in her numerous elegies that she becomes more clearly aligned with the thanatos-eros motif of nineteenth-century romantics than with her eighteenth-century contemporaries. Her poetics of the imagination and the sublime, comprising the fourth representation of freedom, even more strongly attests her romantic alignment. This young poet's intense longing for the spiritual world motivated her to use her poetry as a means of escaping an unsatisfactory, temporal world. The imagination and the sublime become tools by which she accomplishes her short-lived escape. She presents so sophisticated a grasp of these two eighteenth-century aesthetic ideas, which emphatically heralded the romantic movement, that their consideration deserves extended attention.

> John C. Shields, "Phillis Wheatley's Struggle for Freedom in Her Poetry and Prose," *The Collected Works of Phillis Wheatley* (New York: Oxford University Press, 1988), pp. 230–31.

BLYDEN JACKSON   No black poet until Paul Laurence Dunbar in the 1890s was so widely known as Phillis Wheatley, and probably none should have been. She was not only much more a beneficiary of training in literacy than either Lucy Terry or Jupiter Hammon. She was also born, apparently, with more of a native endowment for poetry than either of them. Neoclassicism was the prevailing mode for writers of her time. It was a mode to which she gave a close and conscious allegiance. She was sympathetically acquainted with such Latin poets as Virgil and Ovid, exemplars of the poetic art from classical antiquity whom neoclassicists revered. Milton, incidentally, clearly appealed to her, and Miltonic influences may be detected widely in her work. Even so, Pope, the arch practitioner of English neoclassicism, was her model of models. Of the thirty-nine poems in her *Poems on Various Subjects*, all but five are not only in the neoclassical heroic couplet but also in that particular form of couplet—to the full extent, apparently, of which she was capable—precisely in both the manner and spirit of Pope. Pope preeminently affected satire, often of the most virulent tone and the bitterest, most savage content. Phillis Wheatley—perhaps, it can be conjectured, because of her vulnerable position in society—was one neoclassicist who did not turn to satire. But in every other significant respect, she followed Pope and the neoclassicists religiously. She invoked the muses. She wrote elegies, fourteen in her *Poems on Various Subjects*. She adopted subjects which permitted her to expatiate on abstractions, as in her "On Recollection" and "On Imagination." She indulged rather freely in personification, as became an orthodox neoclassicist, and always in that special neoclassical way which is divided by all too thin a line from abstraction, not because, in it, the process of abstraction has been too personified, but because, in it, the purported process of personification has been too abstract. She was urbane, logical, impersonal in tone (even when writing, as she did in her elegies, of people she knew), and prone to the use of poetic diction— all of these as a good neoclassicist should have been. Her poetry functioned to remind its audience of mankind's universal traits and sentiments and of the occasions in human experience which all men tend to share. Thus, it is axiomatic with her critics that she was an occasional poet, very much in keeping with her neoclassical bent.

> Blyden Jackson, *A History of Afro-American Literature* (Baton Rouge: Louisiana State University Press, 1989), Vol. 1, pp. 42–43

◈ *Bibliography*

An Elegiac Poem, on the Death of That Celebrated Divine, and Eminent Servant
     of Jesus Christ, the Reverend and Learned George Whitefield. 1770.

To Mrs. Leonard on the Death of Her Husband. 1771.

To the Honorable Thomas Hubbard, Esq. on the Death of Mrs. Thankfull Leonard.
     1773.

An Elegy, to Miss Mary Moorhead, on the Death of Her Father, the Rev. Mr. John Moorhead. 1773.

Poems on Various Subjects, Religious and Moral. 1773.

An Elegy, Sacred to the Memory of That Great Divine, the Reverend and Learned Dr. Samuel Cooper. 1784.

Liberty and Peace: A Poem. 1784.

Memoir and Poems of Phillis Wheatley. Ed. Margaretta Matilda Odell. 1834.

Letters. [Ed. Charles Deane.] 1864.

Poems. 1909.

Poems and Letters. Ed. Charles Frederick Heartman. 1915.

Life and Works of Phillis Wheatley. Ed. G. Herbert Renfro. 1916.

Poems. Ed. Charlotte Ruth Wright. 1930.

Poems. Ed. Julian D. Mason, Jr. 1966, 1989.

Collected Works. Ed. John C. Shields. 1988.

Albery Allson Whitman
1851–1901

ALBERY ALLSON WHITMAN was born in slavery on May 30, 1851, on the estate of an unknown farmer near Munfordsville, Kentucky. His mother died when he was eleven and his father died the next year. After the Civil War Whitman, now free, lived variously in Kentucky and Ohio as a laborer and also attended school for seven months. With this learning he was able to become a schoolteacher in Ohio and later in Kentucky. Around 1870 he enrolled at Wilberforce University in Wilberforce, Ohio, but attended only for six months. During his brief stay there, however, he came under the influence of the university's president, Daniel Alexander Payne, whom Whitman considered one of the most important influences upon his life and work.

Payne, who was also a bishop of the African Methodist Episcopal Church, probably encouraged Whitman to enter the ministry, and Whitman became a pastor of A.M.E. churches in Ohio, Kansas, and elsewhere. He remained associated with Wilberforce University, becoming its general financial agent by 1877. At some point Whitman married a woman named Caddie, with whom he had three daughters. These daughters became a successful vaudeville team during the early decades of the twentieth century.

Whitman began writing in the 1870s. His first book, *Essay on the Ten Plagues and Miscellaneous Poems*, was probably published in 1871, but no copies appear to survive. Two years later Whitman issued *Leelah Misled*, a melodramatic poem that does not address racial issues. In 1877 *Not a Man, and Yet a Man* was issued. At 5000 lines it is one of the longest poems ever written by a black American. Although betraying the influence of many of the standard poets of the day, *Not a Man, and Yet a Man* deals vigorously with the evils of slavery and boldly suggests the possibility of interracial love between Rodney, the slave hero of the poem, and Dora, the daughter of Rodney's owner.

Whitman's next major work, *The Rape of Florida* (1884; reissued in a slightly revised edition the following year as *Twasinta's Seminoles; or, Rape*

of Florida), discusses racial issues more indirectly in its account of two
Seminole chiefs, one of whom has some Negro blood. Whitman's last significant volume, *An Idyl of the South* (1901), consists of two long poems in
ottava rima, one of which ("The Octoroon") again broaches the subject of
interracial romance. Some shorter verses by Whitman are appended to *Not
a Man, and Yet a Man*, and the 1893 pamphlet *World's Fair Poem* contains
two short but undistinguished poems.

  Whitman spent the last years of his life as pastor of St. Phillips Church
in Savannah, Georgia, and Allen Temple in Atlanta. While visiting in
Anniston, Alabama, he contracted pneumonia and died on June 29, 1901.
Since his death he has come to be regarded as the leading black American
poet of the nineteenth century.

◈ *Critical Extracts*

DANIEL ALEXANDER PAYNE   Mr. Whitman is by nature a
poet. A classic training and wide travel over his country and foreign lands
might have brought him into high rank among American poets, and may
yet if he will emancipate himself from the bondage of alcoholic drinks. In
both poems may be found some beautiful passages. Listen to these from *Not
a Man*:

> Full blue-eyed Summer, stately coming on,
> With shouting harvests stood the hills upon;
> The breath of wasting juices did inhale,
> With blooming cotton whitened in the vale,
> Spread out the ripened cane along the steep,
> And waving rice-fields in the swamp did reap.

  From *The Rape of Florida* I give a sublime specimen from stanza fifteen,
in Canto I., page 14:

> Have I not seen the hills of Candahar
>   Clothed in the fury of a thunder-storm;
> When Majesty rolled in his cloud-day car,
>   Wreathed his dread brow with lightning's livid form,
> And with a deluge robed his threatening arm;
>   Not seen when Night fled his terrific feet,
> The great deep rose to utter forth alarm,
>   The hills in dreadful hurry rushed to meet,
>   And rocking mountains started from their darkened seat?

O Whitman, Whitman! canst thou not break the chains that bind thee
to the chariot-wheels of intemperance? Why boast of thy freedom from the
white man, and yet be the slave of alcohol?

> Daniel Alexander Payne, *Recollections of Seventy Years* (Nashville, TN: A.M.E. Sunday
> School Union, 1888), pp. 238–39

G. M. McCLELLAN   There are four poets ⟨. . .⟩ who have attracted
much attention and favorable criticism, and of these I will speak in turn.
It is in order to speak of Mr. A. A. Whitman first, because he appeared
first of all and in one particular of excellency he is first of all four. His *Rape
of Florida* is truly poetry and as a *sustained effort,* as an attempt *in great lines,*
it surpasses in true merit anything yet done by a Negro, and this assertion
without one qualifying word. He failed as a poet? Certainly. Mr. Whitman
made attempts in lines in which Shelley, Keats and Spenser triumphed, and
with such mediocrity only possible to him in such a highway, what else could
follow beyond a passing notice, though his *Rape of Florida* is a production of
much more than passing merit. Aside from the mediocrity of the work
attempted in Spenserian lines the man himself in his lack of learning, in
his inexpressible egotism, was derogatory to his ultimate success, and his
styling himself as the William Cullen Bryant of the Negro race was sickening
in the extreme. Mr. Whitman died recently, but not before he had done
all in literary excellence that could be hoped from him. It remains true,
however, that he was worthy of a much better place than is accorded him
as a Negro poet, and it is to be regretted that his work is so little known
among us.

> G. M. McClellan, "The Negro as a Writer," *Twentieth Century Negro Literature,* ed.
> D. W. Culp (Naperville, IL: J. L. Nichols, 1902), pp. 279–80

BENJAMIN BRAWLEY   The work of Whitman himself is exceed-
ingly baffling. It is to his credit that something about his work at once
commands judgment by the highest standards. If we consider it on this basis,
we find that it is diffuse, exhibits many lapses in taste, is faulty metrically,
as if done in haste, and shows imitation on every hand. It imitates Whittier,
Longfellow and Tennyson; Scott, Byron and Moore. "The Old Sac Village"
and "Nanawawa's Suitors" are very evidently *Hiawatha* over again, and
"Custer's Last Ride" is simply another version of "The Charge of the Light

Brigade." And yet, whenever one has about decided that Whitman is not worthy of consideration, the poet insists on a revision of judgment; and he certainly could not have imitated so many writers so readily, if he had not had some solid basis in appreciation. ⟨. . .⟩

In 1890 Whitman brought out an edition of *Not a Man and Yet a Man* and *The Rape of Florida*, adding to these a collection of miscellaneous poems, *Drifted Leaves*, and in 1901 he published *An Idyl of the South*, an epic poem in two parts. It is to be regretted that he did not have the training that comes from the best university education. He had the taste and the talent to benefit from such culture in the greatest degree.

> Benjamin Brawley, "Three Negro Poets: Horton, Mrs. Harper, and Whitman," *Journal of Negro History* 2, No. 4 (October 1917): 388–91

VERNON LOGGINS   *Not a Man, and Yet a Man* contains more than two hundred and fifty closely printed pages, and is therefore to be classed among the more lengthy American poems. As a work of metrical imitations it is a veritable *tour de force*, reverting back in its effect to an eighteenth-century American poem, Timothy Dwight's *Greenfield Hill*, which Whitman probably did not know. In easy couplets which seem to repeat rather than echo the music of Goldsmith's *The Deserted Village*, the opening of the poem introduces us to Rodney, a heroic slave, the property of Sir Maxey, the richest man in a town of the Middle West, called Saville, where life is pioneer and yet idyllic. We are next taken to an Indian village, in reading the description of which we might almost be deceived into believing that we hear the exact trochaics of Longfellow's *Hiawatha*. In verse following Whittier's "Snow-Bound" and Longfellow's "Paul Revere's Ride," we are told of how Sir Maxey's daughter, Dora, is taken captive by the Indians, of how Rodney rescues her and wins her affections, and of how her father, outraged at the thought of her love for his black slave, scorns the promise which he had made to give her as wife to the man who would save her from her captors. Rodney is turned over to a slave trader to be sold into the far South. We next find him on a plantation in Florida, where he forgets his infatuation for Dora in a real love, that for Leona, a Creole slave. After a stirring chain of events, the slave lovers win their way to Canada and freedom. The happenings in Florida are told in the measures of Scott's *Lady of the Lake*, scarcely disguised even in such occasional dialect passages as the following:

> In yonder room is Rodney tied,
> Where stands a locust on dis side.
> De white folks sell him in de morn,
> An' he'll be left yer, shore's yer born,
> Go see him, gal, bid him farewell,
> An' tell him what yer's got to tell,
> An' I'll stand here, de outside by,
> An' keep watchout wid open eye.

The conclusion, in the hexameters of Longfellow's *Evangeline*, shows Rodney and Leona in Canada, where chance throws them under the protection of Dora, who has discovered that what she had interpreted as love for Rodney was after all admiration for his heroism and sympathy for his lot. Because the varying music of so many well-known unrelated poems is incorporated in it, *Not a Man, and Yet a Man* seems complicated. The plot is in reality well unified, and the characterization is adequately consistent.

Vernon Loggins, *The Negro Author: His Development in America to 1900* (New York: Columbia University Press, 1931), pp. 337–38

KENNY J. WILLIAMS   Whitman admitted the influence of Byron and Spenser ⟨in *Not a Man, and Yet a Man*⟩, but it appears from the poem that his knowledge of Spenser was a second-hand one for his use of the nine-line Spenserian stanza is more reminiscent in tone of Byron than of Spenser. In an apologetic dedicatory statement which appears in *The Rape of Florida*, Whitman interestingly analyzed his own work.

> [Concerning] the 'stately verse,' mastered only by Spenser, Byron, and a very few other great poets, I may seem to have 'rushed in where angels fear to tread.' To this view of the matter, I will say by way of defense: some Negro's sure to do everything that any one else has ever done, and as none of the race have executed a poem in the 'stately verse,' I simply *venture in*.

It would be advantageous to discover exactly how extensive was Whitman's actual reading background. As a student at Wilberforce he was probably exposed to the literary masters; yet, it becomes extremely difficult to ascertain how much he is indebted to them if at all. There is enough originality in all of his work to preclude any conscious imitation. On the other hand, in *Not a Man, and Yet a Man* there appear to be traces of Dwight's *Greenfield Hill* in the celebration of the countryside as well as of Goldsmith's *The Deserted Village*. When he describes the Indian settlement, Whitman seems to approximate Longfellow. Even vestiges of Scott's *The Lady of the Lake* seem discernible. Whitman may have had an excellent ear for poetic sound and may have absorbed the popular works of his period. In spite of the fact that he may have incorporated the sounds which he liked best into his own work, *Not a Man, and Yet a Man* is an exciting adventure story which is indicative of the sustained poetic powers of Whitman. While Dora and her father are stereotypes, both Rodney and Leona emerge as warmly human creations. Rodney, whose story unifies the entire work, is far more believable than the usual romantic hero in a work of this nature.

> Kenny J. Williams, *They Also Spoke: An Essay on Negro Literature in America 1787–1930* (Nashville, TN: Townsend Press, 1970), pp. 139–40

LOUIS D. RUBIN, JR.   Under other circumstances, he might have achieved considerable fame, for the best of his work is not notably inferior to the leading American poetry of the latter years of the nineteenth century. But unfortunately for Whitman's reputation, he wrote at a time when there was little or no audience for a black poet who would deal boldly with the unlovely circumstance of the black American. Now that the Civil War was done, the zeal for abolition had abated and it was no longer considered appropriate to publish protest poems by black poets. The era of reconciliation between North and South was underway, and in order for that reconciliation to take place, it was necessary to overlook the uncomfortable fact that the freedman was being increasingly forced into a position of peonage in the post-Reconstruction South. Thus a poem such as *Twasinta's Seminoles* made uncomfortable reading, while *Not a Man, and Yet a Man*, which in abolitionist times would doubtless have created a considerable sensation, went without a wide audience. The nation had wearied of the black man's troubles; it did not wish to be reminded that the Civil War had left him far from free. In Whitman's instance this meant that a poet of decided gifts went unnoticed. For a black poet to achieve literary fame, therefore, a different kind of talent was required; the strident note of protest must give way to something more oblique and artful. By the time of Whitman's death, in 1902, the black poet who could provide that had already arrived on the scene. He was Paul Laurence Dunbar.

> Louis D. Rubin, Jr., "The Search for Language, 1746–1923," *Black Poetry in America: Two Essays in Historical Interpretation* by Blyden Jackson and Louis D. Rubin, Jr. (Baton Rouge: Louisiana State University Press, 1974), pp. 12–13

JOAN R. SHERMAN   "Poetry," Whitman wrote ⟨in *The Rape of Florida*⟩, "is the language of universal sentiment. . . . Her voice is the voice of Eternity dwelling in all great souls. Her aims are the inducements of Heaven, and her triumphs the survival of the Beautiful, the True, and the Good." His critical theory echoes Poe, and much of his poetry steps to the measures of Longfellow, Byron, Tennyson, Whittier, and Scott. But Albery A. Whitman had no less the ear for music, the eye for beauty, and the soul of these poets. He wished to emulate them but lacked their disciplined craftsmanship developed through long, secure years of apprenticeship and education he never knew. Twelve years a slave, Whitman transformed himself by manual labor and force of mind and will from a pauper farmboy into a respected minister and the poet hero of his race. Despite only a year of formal schooling, he became thoroughly conversant with the celebrated English and American poets he naturally adopted as models of "the Beautiful, the True, and the Good." Much of Whitman's poetry is technically weak and diffuse, marred by careless versification, burdened with overblown rhetoric and didactic digressions. However, he did supremely well with what he had: a sure dramatic sense, a talent for suspenseful narration, romantic description, communication of pathos, irony, and lovers' emotions, and the courage to attempt difficult meters and epic-length poems. Above all, he had a sense of honor, race pride, and a code of manliness which his poetry urged on all who struggled for racial progress. In the twenty-eight years from *Leelah Misled* to "The Octoroon," Whitman's talent matured, his intellectual and emotional responses deepened, and his technical skills improved. ⟨. . .⟩

It is uncertain whether Albery Whitman or Frances E. W. Harper was the more prolific black poet of their century, considering the lady's twenty-three-year head start. Quantity aside, Mrs. Harper won acclaim as a prophet in her own country and enjoyed all spiritual and financial rewards of popularity. She had no need to plead for recognition, as Whitman does in "A Question":

> Shall my hand lie cold on the strings of my lyre,
> And the heart that is warm lose its pathos and fire,
>   Ere my countrymen hear my song?
> Shall the bard who sings in the tents of the slave,
> And now wakes his harp for the free and the brave,
>   Unheeded wander along?

For Mrs. Harper poetry was consciously a tool: she wrote "songs for the people" to uplift them, save their souls, and reform their habits. For Albery Whitman, on the other hand, poetry was "survival of the Beautiful": he wrote poems because he loved poetry and cherished an ideal of art for art's

sake and for the sake of proving the race's creative talent. Preaching, however, came naturally to him—it was his vocation. Thus the beautiful suffers
adulteration whenever Whitman cannot resist his justifiable pride in "a
little learning" and a large intelligence. But unlike Mrs. Harper and their
contemporaries, he does not burden the poetry with many "Thou shalts"
and "shalt nots." His atypical Christianity disdains ritual and dogma to sing
God in Nature, love between man and woman, and the free mind's eternal
power. Like another Whitman (although with greater inhibitions and far
less talent), this good black poet celebrates himself, hymns the bard as seer
and the oneness of all body and soul.

Albery Whitman's poetry is not utilitarian, which sets him apart from
all his fellow poets with a cause. Although he exalts manliness and insists
on race loyalty, he generally avoids accusatory polemic as well as sentimental
and self-pitying rhetoric. Whitman escapes the influence of Booker T.
Washington's ideology, and he avoids utopianizing life on the old plantation
in dialect verse. His work is rather an attempt at full-blown Romantic
poetry, looking back to legendary pastoral worlds—clearly marred by race
prejudice, seeing the present as a sphere of unlimited human potentiality,
and looking forward to an ideal earth perfected by human love and poetic
genius. Whitman's egoism and his tendency to express any and every flut-
tering of his heart in verse bind him even closer to the effusive Romantic
poets, while the allegorical dimensions of his work separate him further
from black poets of his era. Whatever a line count may reveal, by aesthetic
standards of any age Whitman was a better poet than Mrs. Harper. Moreover,
his poetry offers more profound perceptions and a more catholic range of
subjects and versification than the laureate Dunbar's lyrics. Albery Whitman
dared to be an innovator and a "fearless manly man" in his poetry. All
obstacles considered, his was a splendid ambition and a considerable achievement.

Joan R. Sherman, "Albery Allson Whitman," *Invisible Poets: Afro-Americans of the
Nineteenth Century* (Urbana: University of Illinois Press, 1974), pp. 116–17, 126–27

CARL L. MARSHALL   Although Albery A. Whitman has received
critical notice as the best Black American poet before Dunbar, he has not
been clearly seen as a writer of protest poetry. Yet his idealistic themes, his
literary forms, and his elevated diction, as well as his direct statements,
reveal his opposition to the inferior status that America sought to impose
on him. Unfortunately, Whitman wrote at a time (after the Reconstruction

Period) when there was little or no audience for a Black poet who disregarded dialect verse and dealt with the harsh realities of Afro-American life. Not only the old abolitionist zeal but also the support and encouragement formerly given to aspiring writers had vanished. America, intent on the gospel of wealth and reconciliation of North and South, disdained and ignored strident notes of protest. Apparently, Whitman found a sympathetic ear only when he gave platform-readings. None the less, this poet and practicing minister, who transcended his slave birth in Kentucky and scanty formal education at Troy, Ohio, and Wilberforce University, spoke out defiantly.

In his long narrative poems, *Not a Man and Yet a Man* (1877) and *The Rape of Florida* (1884), Whitman expressed strong racial feelings. He used introductory passages, dedications, plots, and digressions from his stories to convey sentiments echoed by other articulate Black men in pulpit and press, classroom and convention hall. Notwithstanding his use of idealized heroes of mixed or Indian blood, Whitman never lets his readers forget his profound belief in freedom and equality for his race. ⟨. . .⟩

Albery Whitman was a latter-day romantic, intrigued by the world of literature and the world of ideals. Clearly he was at his poetic best in treating love, beauty, honor, adventure, and the delights of nature. But neither his deep inclinations nor the exigencies of earning a living as a minister in the African Methodist Episcopal Church prevented him from denouncing and resisting the subjugation of his race. He expressed militant ideas that ally him with illustrious forerunners and with contemporaries like T. Thomas Fortune. His emphasis on self-trust, education, and full civil and political rights made him a worthy herald of W. E. B. Du Bois. In these poems Whitman is a voice of spirited racial protest.

Carl L. Marshall, "Two Protest Poems by Albery A. Whitman," *CLA Journal* 19, No. 1 (September 1975): 50–51, 56

DICKSON D. BRUCE, JR.   Whitman's self-consciousness as a poet was well shown in his introduction to *The Rape of Florida*, where he discussed his ideas about poetry, about his role as a poet, and about racial questions. Whitman stoutly defended the importance of poetry and poets, to a great extent in ways that were compatible with others' genteel ideas about literature. He argued that poetry had a special connection with truth, and that truth itself was founded on beauty, goodness, and sentiment. And he saw the poet's mission as one of setting forth the proper feelings—what Mrs. Washington called the "best affections."

But Whitman went beyond sentimental ideals in his understanding of literature, and even beyond the ideological directions outlined by Douglass and his colleagues. Whitman's understanding of the function of literature grew out of his more general perceptions of himself as an individual. One gets a sense of these perceptions from an autobiographical passage in the introduction. "I was in bondage," Whitman wrote. "*I never was a slave,—* the infamous laws of a savage despotism took my substance—what of that? Many a man has lost all he had, except his manhood." Whitman was deeply concerned with freedom and manhood and with what might be considered a psychological resistance to racism. At one point in the poem itself, he has one of his characters declare: "The good, the great, and the true, are, if so, born, / And so with slaves, *chains could not make the slave.*" Whitman believed that poetry could allow the poet to make a similar psychological stand against oppression. "Poesy is free," he wrote, "and not for hire." From his point of view, writing poetry provided an individual with an opportunity to experience psychological freedom, even in the face of the worst racial oppression.

No one else in this period came to terms with the psychological dimension of literary work so clearly as Whitman. No one else so fully described literature as a way to achieve at least a momentary transcendence over a racist society. But Whitman's view of poetry was a psychological complement to the ideological orientation of virtually all black writing from this period. Producing literature was generally seen as a way of fighting prejudice by proving black character. In his remarks, Whitman added a level of meaning that was implied by more ideological views of what literature could do— pointing to a satisfaction that other writers may have felt but never put into words.

His great self-consciousness makes all the more significant the fact that Whitman was, in most ways, as conservative as other black writers of his era. It is hard to quarrel with the modern assessment that, as a poet, Whitman was an excellent craftsman who admired good poetry and sought to equal it himself rather than to create much that was new. Sterling Brown, in 1939, described him as one of the "mocking-bird school of poets." On the whole, this meant that Whitman did not depart far from the main poetic fashions of his day in either form or theme. His newspaper and magazine pieces tended to deal with such familiar topics as evangelical piety and the sentimental beauties of nature. His shorter works on racial questions were no less carefully circumscribed. His 1893 poem "The Freedman's Triumphant Song" extolled the patriotism of black Americans and celebrated their contributions to American life and history. Indulging in some ugly anti-immigrant sentiment, Whitman concluded the poem with an optimistically voiced plea to white America to recognize "One land: the best by mortals ever trod; / One flag, one people, and one father—God." ⟨. . .⟩

When one looks at Whitman's poetry, one is looking at work that reached the limits of ambition in the black literary community during the period between the close of Reconstruction and the mid-1890s, when Paul Laurence Dunbar's writing, in particular, would change the course of black literature. Whitman reached these limits with his ambitious scope and his self-conscious stress on technique. But he remained within them by never moving beyond what, in polite circles, would be considered good poetry.

As Whitman's work reveals, then, the creative energies of black writers could be channeled in only a few directions. In terms of form, they could go only toward existing forms, or at most in the direction of the ambitious use of received forms, as in Whitman's poetry. Thematically, the constraints were still tighter. There were approved ways of talking about racial questions, a point emphasized by the extent to which the self-conscious, ambitious Whitman, no less than other black writers, stuck with them.

Dickson D. Bruce, Jr., *Black American Writing from the Nadir: The Evolution of a Literary Tradition 1877–1915* (Baton Rouge: Louisiana State University Press, 1989), pp. 34–35, 37

BLYDEN JACKSON   Whitman's interest in Florida did not cease with *Not a Man*. He returned to the once-Spanish colony for *The Rape of Florida*, or *Twasinta's Seminoles*, under either name essentially the same poem. The Indian chief, a Seminole, in *The Rape of Florida* who matches Pashepaho of *Not a Man* as a figure of reverence among his people is named Palmecho. Incidentally, the fabled Osceola does appear in *The Rape of Florida*, but only momentarily and certainly not to his own best advantage. Like Pashepaho and Sir Maxey, Palmecho has a beautiful daughter, the tawny Ewald, through whose veins flows a mixture of Indian, Spanish, and Negro blood. Ewald loves, and is loved by, the young Seminole chief Atlassa, in all respects except his lack of Negro blood a counterpart of Rodney from *Not a Man*. The black presence, indeed, in *The Rape of Florida* is even less than in *Not a Man*. Ewald alone of the major characters in the later poem has a touch of Negro ancestry. Yet, in an important way, *The Rape of Florida* is but an extension of *Not a Man*. A quest for freedom dominates the lives of Palmecho, Ewald, and Atlassa and serves as the theme for their poem as, in *Not a Man*, it had dominated the life of Rodney and served as the theme of his poem.

Whitman chose to write *The Rape of Florida* in the Spenserian stanza, the first black poet to be so bold. The poem is less than half as long as *Not a Man*, by no means an indication that it is short (which it is not). Its 257 stanzas are divided into 4 cantos. From first almost to last, it tells a tale of white aggression and perfidy. Its main action begins when an American military force, capitalizing on surprise, attacks Palmecho's village, in the process wounding Palmecho. It may be interesting to note, in view of the record of the Seminoles in actual history, that Whitman attributes to the Seminoles, unless provoked, a taste for peaceful coexistence not unlike that which he had earlier attributed to Pashepaho's people. Palmecho and his people are saved by fellow Seminoles, led by Atlassa, who rush to Palmecho's aid and put to flight the American soldiers. Nevertheless, Palmecho does fall all too soon again into American hands. Under a flag of truce, which he foolishly trusts, he attends a peace conference with the Americans in St. Augustine, where they once more imprison him. Ewald, quite to the contrary, eludes the Americans, who had planned to capture her also, and turns to Atlassa for protection. He places her, he thinks, out of harm's way, in his own village and, with the help of two of his braves, for a second time rescues her father, only to discover, when he returns home, that the Americans now have Ewald. Further conflict between the Seminoles and the Americans is, in a manner, resolved when the Americans, who obtain Palmecho now for a third time, herd the Seminoles and black maroons whom they have not killed onto a ship which is to go to Mexico. The Seminoles and maroons leave Florida in chains. The captain of their transport, however, unchains them. He is more humane than their American captors. Landed in Mexico, they attempt there to start a new life.

The Rape of Florida does not end so happily as *Not a Man*. Yet Atlassa, Ewald, and their comrades in Mexico are free and do have, although they have little else, in their freedom a chance to begin a new life. Carl Marshall, the leading exponent of the thesis that Whitman has been too summarily underestimated by critics as a writer of racial protest, has studied carefully *The Rape of Florida*. Marshall finds ample protest in the poem. He concedes that Whitman is a romantic—a "latter-day romantic." But, to him, Whitman is far from an unthinking romantic. According to Marshall, Whitman conceived of nature as a symbol and, indeed, as such (while Marshall does not say this explicitly), of a kind which permits it to be, in ways discernible to man, if only he troubles himself enough to see what it is possible to perceive, an expression of God's attributes and will. We may wish to remember here

Whitman's love of the country—of his external surroundings sheerly as substances of themselves—in the part of Kentucky where he was born and to parallel that love with the feeling for similar aspects of his environment so ardently enunciated by Wordsworth in such poems of his as *The Prelude* and "Tintern Abbey." Neither Whitman nor Wordsworth believed that nature could be as it was without significance for man. Both saw in nature a book, as it were, written by a divine hand, containing knowledge of the utmost importance for men who wanted to live their lives under the most favorable of circumstances. Both, too, saw in nature incontrovertible proofs that God and his universe are ultimately benevolent as well as beautiful. So, Marshall asserts that, for Whitman, nature possessed the power of promoting man's highest qualities, none of which, Marshall further asserts, in Whitman's view, appeared to nature of greater consequence than freedom of the mind.

> Blyden Jackson, *A History of Afro-American Literature* (Baton Rouge: Louisiana State University Press, 1989), Vol. 1, pp. 285–86

▩ *Bibliography*

Essay on the Ten Plagues and Miscellaneous Poems. c. 1871. Lost.

Leelah Misled. 1873.

Not a Man, and Yet a Man. 1877.

The Rape of Florida. 1884, 1885 (as *Twasinta's Seminoles; or, Rape of Florida*).

Twasinta's Seminoles; Not a Man and Yet a Man; Drifted Leaves: A Collection of Poems. 1890.

World's Fair Poem. 1893.

An Idyl of the South: An Epic Poem in Two Parts. 1901.